# Classified

by
## E. Bly Beamesderfer

**TEACH Services, Inc.**
P U B L I S H I N G
www.TEACHServices.com • (800) 367-1844

Copyright © 2013 TEACH Services, Inc.
ISBN-13: 978-1-57258-813-4 (Paperback)
ISBN-13: 978-1-57258-814-1 (Hardback)
ISBN-13: 978-1-57258-815-8 (Epub)
ISBN-13: 978-1-57258-816-5 (Kindle)

Library of Congress Control Number: 2012956211

Published by

**TEACH Services, Inc.**
P U B L I S H I N G
www.TEACHServices.com ● (800) 367-1844

# Table of Contents

# Preface

This book is a compilation of many of my impressions and has spanned over ten years in preparation, seemingly not meant to be completed before the fullness of time. I share my impressions as encouragement for Christians who may have lost their way and feel they have no recourse left but to remain disconnected from God, as well as for those who have maintained a connection with God but have been separated from the church body. Ephesians 1:22, 23 tells us Christ is the "head over all things to the church, which is his body." Ephesians 5:23 confirms this and also states that Christ "is the Savior of the body" (NKJV). Does this mean we must be members of the church body in order to be connected with Christ, the head, to receive salvation? Are there exceptions to this teaching? Who or what is the church? Is there salvation apart from the body? How are we classified?

It is my prayer that this book will encourage you to be classified as a member of the body of Christ and to receive His salvation.

*Bly Beamesderfer*

# Chapter One

# **One Flesh**

"If I were the devil, if I were the prince of darkness, I'd want to engulf the whole world in darkness. I would have a third of its real estate and four-fifths of its population, but I wouldn't be happy until I had seized the ripest apple on the tree, thee. So I would set about however necessary to take over the United States. I'd subvert the churches first. I'd begin with a campaign of whispers. With the wisdom of a serpent, I would whisper to you as I whispered to Eve, 'Do as you please.'

"To the young, I would whisper that the Bible is a myth. I would convince them that man created God instead of the other way around. I would confide that, what is bad is good and what is good is 'square.'

"And the old, I would teach to pray after me, 'Our Father, which art in Washington.' And then, I'd get organized.

"I'd educate authors in how to make lurid literature exciting so that anything else would appear dull and uninteresting. I'd threaten TV with dirtier movies and visa versa. I'd peddle narcotics to whom I could. I'd sell alcohol to ladies and gentlemen of distinction. I'd tranquilize the rest with pills.

"If I were the devil, I'd soon have families at war with themselves, churches at war with themselves, and nations at war with themselves, until each in its turn was consumed.

"And with promises of higher ratings, I'd have mesmerizing media fanning the flames.

"If I were the devil, I would encourage schools to refine young intellects but neglect to discipline emotions; just let those run wild until before you knew it, you'd have to have drug-sniffing dogs and metal detectors at every schoolhouse door.

"Within a decade, I'd have prisons overflowing. I'd have judges promoting pornography. Soon I could evict God from the courthouse, and then from the schoolhouse, and then from the house of congress. And in His own churches I would substitute psychology for religion and deify science. I would lure priests and pastors into misusing boys and girls and church money.

"If I were the devil, I'd make the symbol of Easter an egg and the symbol of Christmas a bottle.

"If I were the devil, I would take from those who have and I would give to those who wanted, until I had killed the incentive of the ambitious. And what do you bet I couldn't get the whole states to promote gambling as the way to get rich. I would caution against extremes in hard work, in patriotism, in moral conduct.

"I would convince the young that marriage is old fashioned, that swinging is more fun, that what you see on TV is the way to be, and thus I could undress you in public, and I could lure you into bed with diseases for which there is no cure.

"In other words, If I were the devil, I'd just keep right on doing what he's doing" (Paul Harvey, "If I Were the Devil," 1965).

Satan has been doing his work very skillfully and successfully. Looking back in the 1960s and 1970s, people were joining trendy activist movements trying to discover something real and exciting in or about their lives. A very popular movement at the time was the hippy culture. This movement especially attracted young people leaving home. Maybe these young people thought it was cool to be different, or maybe they were trying to find themselves. But nonetheless, they were against the establishment and believed that society was being led astray by a crooked government. This philosophy was labeled antiestablishmentarianism. Whatever the reason for the hippies' searching today we find the establishment here and the hippies gone.

Perhaps none of this has to do with Christianity, but perhaps it does. A parallel can be found in today's disruption of home and society and the search for total happiness. Similarly, there is a correlation between the turmoil in the home and what has happened in the church, which ultimately affects the finishing work of God and personal salvation.

It seems Satan has shifted gears from the world to the church. If we look at what is occurring in the church today, we can see a similar phenomenon taking place. We see many believers displaying the same attitude of dissatisfaction and wanting to discover something new and exciting in this world. They say the establishment is corrupt and we need to disconnect ourselves with it. They flatter themselves by separating from the establishment and crying out, "We are the chosen ones, the 144,000, the called-out, the remnant!" Or, "We are those without spot or wrinkle, we have new light," they shout. And so they begin their independent ministry to convince others they must leave the main body or be rejected by Christ. But let's take a closer look at what is really happening with these people.

First of all, we need to understand that not all independent ministries are destructive. Many ministries are powerfully constructive and supportive of the main body. However, there are also independent unions that are in opposition to the main body; consequently, these alliances and their reputations are giving a bad name to all ministries. The impression one gets upon hearing the words *self-supporting* or *independent* is *separation*. One reason for this thought process is that the words *independent* or *self-supporting* suggest *opposition*. Anytime a person takes the word *supporting* and precedes it with *self-* or takes the word *dependent* and precedes it with *I* (*In*), the obvious conclusion is *separation* in this context, unless you are in dependence on Christ.

The Bible teaches there is one faith and one body of which we are all members and of which the Holy Spirit gives special gifts so that the members can be strengthened (Rom. 12:3–5; 1 Cor. 12:11–13; Eph. 4:3–5). But when we bring in the selfish I's, it causes separation in the body. We need to look, rather, for the *dependently supportive* ministries of the body.

One of Christ's greatest concerns for us in the last days is for us to take heed that no one deceives us because many will come proclaiming to be Jesus. Even the elect ones will have trouble distinguishing the false from the true. The elect are His remnant.

In Matthew 24:4, 5, 24, Jesus states:

> Take heed that no man deceive you. For many shall come in my name, saying, I am Christ; and shall deceive many.... For there shall arise false Christs, and false prophets, and shall shew great signs and wonders; insomuch that, if it were possible, they shall deceive the very elect.

Here Jesus warns us not to be followers of people who are teaching things contrary to or against the body, of which Christ is the head. Remember, there can be only one remnant. If there be another remnant, we must conclude that it is a deception.

Jesus, through His Word, teaches there is one truth, one body, and one remnant. Revelation 12:17 clearly acknowledges a single remnant: "And the dragon was wroth with the woman, and went to make war with the remnant of her seed, which keep the commandments of God, and have the testimony of Jesus Christ." Revelation 19:10 goes on to tell us that the church that keeps the laws of God and the testimony of

Jesus Christ also carries the spirit of prophecy.

At this point let us consider this question: What does the gift of prophecy have to do with the destiny of the church? Ephesians 4 answers this question, particularly verses 11–14: "And he gave some, apostles, and some, prophets; and some evangelists, and some pastors and teachers; For the perfecting of the saints, for the work of the ministry, for the edifying of the body of Christ." Please notice the reasons these gifts are given: for perfecting (or equipping) the saints and for the edifying (or building up) of the body of Christ.

**Pause now:** Open the Bible to 1 Corinthians 12, read about the "body parts," and especially note verse 18, where it says that God is in charge and does what pleases Him. If you are someone who at one time accepted Jesus as the head of your life, then you are one of His body parts. How are you classified? Are you attached or detached? Are you active or inactive?

Now back to Ephesians 4:13: "Till we all come in the unity of the faith, and of the knowledge of the Son of God, unto a perfect man, unto the measure of the stature of the fulness of Christ." The true remnant will expose itself by demonstrating all the gifts given by the Spirit. If you are a body member, you have received a gift. Are you experiencing that gift, or is it lying dormant? Please give your best to the Master.

At this point notice that God did not just give apostles, prophets, evangelists, pastors, or teachers to His remnant church. He gave all these gifts and more to His last remaining people to arm them for the works of service (ministry) and the unity of the body (church or bride) of Christ.

Of the various groups within the entire Christian community one could be associated with today, how many possess all of these heavenly gifts, including the gift of prophecy? How many keep all of God's ten commandments? The answer is obvious and makes a loud statement as to whom Christ still identifies as His Body, Bride, and remnant.

The gift of prophecy came to the church through Ellen G. White as an endowment bestowed upon His remnant church. It is a gift that God gave as an identifying mark of His church. The groups of this church that separate *themselves* as independent, dissenting factions do not possess the gift of prophecy. They are borrowing it from the true body, or bride, of Christ. Consequently, what they grasp is a false movement of a false remnant; even though they may teach and sound 99.9 percent pure, what they are actually doing is rejecting Christ because they deny His body, and bride. Incidentally, the bride has not yet come to perfect unity and fullness in Christ. But, praise God, the fullness will take place before Jesus arrives because that is why the gifts were given to His remnant. We will be prepared through unity with the Holy Spirit and also through persecution.

Jesus knows the deplorable condition of His bride:

> I know thy works, that thou are neither cold nor hot: I would thou wert cold or hot. So then because thou are lukewarm, and neither cold nor hot, I will spew thee out of my mouth. Because thou sayest, I am rich, and increased with goods, and have need of nothing; and knowest not that thou art wretched, and miserable, and poor, and blind, and naked. (Rev. 3:15–17)

Jesus is calling for a separation from the world, not from the church. He is pleading for repentance, reformation, and revival. He wants us to overcome a do-it-yourself religion. "As many as I love, I rebuke and chasten: be zealous therefore, and repent" (Rev. 3:19). God loves all of us and does not want to see anyone perish. Even though the body as a whole can be classified as lukewarm, you as an individual do not have to be. The antidote to this condition is repentance. Is there a need in your life to be reclassified?

Listen now, here is the punch line in Ephesians 4:14–16:

> That we henceforth be no more children, tossed to and
> fro, and carried about with every wind of doctrine, by
> the sleight of men, and cunning craftiness, whereby
> they lie in wait to deceive; But speaking the truth in
> love, may grow up into him in all things, which is the
> head, even Christ: From whom the whole body fitly
> joined together and compacted by that which every
> joint supplieth, according to the effectual working in
> the measure of every part, maketh increase of the body
> unto the edifying of itself in love.

Here the words *joined together* and *every joint supplieth* cannot be emphasized enough.

If one could look into the innermost workings of the ministries of the separated ones and even into the lives of many of the individuals who run them, one would realize that the same criticisms they had of the body (church) could be true of them. If only we were to follow the council of Ephesians 4:29: "Let no corrupt communication proceed out of your mouth, but that which is good to the use of edifying, that it may minister grace unto the hearers." If we were to follow that advice, how different our outlooks would be.

Too often people want to do the work for God and not the work of God by trying to expose and banish all that is evil, and if they cannot reveal the corrupt, they give up, separate themselves, and group the whole body with Babylon. Could it be we have too many Christ impersonators and not enough Christlike characters? Remember, Jesus said, "Many will come in my name, saying, I am Christ" (Matt. 24:5), which extends to those claiming to do His work! Jesus asks us to be His witnesses, not His prosecutors.

Two parables are instructive in our discussion about separation and classification. In the parable of the wheat and the tares, Christ explains why one cannot classify others' allegiance prematurely:

> Another parable put He forth unto them, saying, The kingdom of heaven is likened unto a man which sowed good seed in his field: but while men slept, his enemy came and sowed tares among the wheat, and went his way. But when the blade was sprung up, and brought forth fruit, then appeared the tares also. So the servants of the householder came and said unto him, Sir, didst not thou sow good seed in thy field? from whence then hath it tares? He said unto them, An enemy hath done this. The servants said unto him, Wilt thou then that we go and gather them up? But he said, Nay; lest while ye gather up the tares, ye root up also the wheat with them. Let both grow together until the harvest: and in the time of harvest I will say to the reapers, Gather ye together first the tares, and bind them in bundles to burn them: but gather the wheat into my barn. (Matt. 13:24–30)

We must remember that we grow together until the harvest, and the only one who does the separating is Christ, the head of the body (bride). Note also, it was while the men (church) slept that the enemy sowed the tares.

In the parable of the ten virgins, the virgins represent the remnant people of God just before Jesus returns to earth.

> Then shall the kingdom of heaven be likened unto ten virgins, which took their lamps, and went forth to meet the bridegroom. And five of them were wise,

and five were foolish. They that were foolish took their lamps, and took no oil with them: But the wise took oil in their vessels with their lamps. While the bridegroom tarried, they all slumbered and slept. And at midnight there was a cry made, Behold, the bridegroom cometh; go ye out to meet him. Then all those virgins arose, and trimmed their lamps. And the foolish said unto the wise, Give us of your oil; for our lamps are gone out. But the wise answered, saying, Not so; lest there be not enough for us and you: but go ye rather to them that sell, and buy for yourselves. And while they went to buy, the bridegroom came; and they that were ready went in with him to the marriage: and the door was shut. Afterward came also the other virgins, saying, Lord, Lord, open to us. But he answered and said, Verily I say unto you, I know you not. Watch therefore, for ye know neither the day nor the hour wherein the Son of man Cometh. (Matt. 25:1–13)

We can draw several lessons from both parables. Notice that all ten virgins are asleep before the loud cry is given, and only half of them enter into the marriage. Both the tares and the foolish virgins lose out on being united with the Maker. Also notice that in both parables, people are not the ones who have the authority to do the separating; circumstances lead up to it. It is the Lord who selects the people who should enter the gateway. In the parable of the wheat and the tares, it is the reapers (angels) who, at the sower's (God's) command, perform the gathering and separating of the harvest. Also, another very important thought here is that it is the tares that are separated from—or removed from among—the wheat, rather than the wheat from the tares; so think twice before you separate yourself from what is going into the barn.

Dear reader, if you expect to live until Jesus returns to earth, then that is the event for which you need to watch and be ready. If you should die before He returns, then that is the event for which you need to be ready. Then, when He returns, you will be resurrected to be with Him at the wedding feast. How do you classify your relationship with Him now? Are you a trimmed and burning light for Him? God's true remnant people will not only have the real gift of prophecy but also keep all ten commandments of God: "And the dragon was wroth with the woman, and went to make war with the remnant of her seed, which keep the commandments of God, and have the testimony of Jesus Christ" (Rev. 12:17). The testimony of Jesus is the spirit of prophecy (Rev.19:10). Obviously, there are some who do not keep the laws of God, which leads to the question, How are the separated, self-supporting, or independent ones not keeping the commandments of God? In order to answer this question, we must first look at what the commandments really do. They reveal sin in our lives the way a mirror reveals dirt on our face. Sin is "the transgression of the law" (1 John 3:4), and it separates (yes, there is that word again) us from God. In order not to be separated from God, we need to belong to His remnant body and keep His commandments once we understand their importance.

**Pause now:** Look at the Ten Commandments, found in Exodus 20:1–17.

Many times we refer to the remnant as having a marriage relationship with God. Can you conclude which one of the last six commandments, if not obeyed, will separate us from our physical marriage? If you guessed the seventh commandment, which states we should not commit adultery, then you are correct.

Can you speculate which of the first four commandments can separate us from God in our spiritual marriage? The answer is in the very first commandment, "Thou shalt have no other gods before me"

(Exod. 20:3). The second commandment tells us, "God is a jealous God" (verse 5).

Who is at the head of the body (bride)? What if we are separated or divorced from God? If we are divided from the body, then we are at odds with the head. No matter what form of godliness one possesses, one has committed spiritual adultery by rejecting the body (bride) of Jesus; and in rejecting the bride, one rejects also the groom because together, the bride and groom are bonded in unity. Genesis 2:24 states, "Therefore shall a man leave his father and his mother and shall cleave unto his wife: and they shall be one flesh." The bride (body) and groom (Christ) are one, inseparable.

To illustrate the connection between a husband and wife, between Christ and the church, the apostle Paul states in Ephesians 5:28–32:

> So ought men to love their wives as their own bodies.
> He that loveth his wife loveth himself. For no man ever
> yet hated his own flesh; but nourisheth and cherisheth
> it, even as the Lord the church: For we are members of
> his body, of his flesh, and of his bones. For this cause
> shall a man leave his father and mother, and shall be
> joined unto his wife, and they two shall be one flesh.
> This is a great mystery: but I speak concerning Christ
> and the church.

Similarly, Paul also writes: "For as the body is one, and hath many members, and all the members of that one body, being many, are one body: so also is Christ" (1 Cor. 12:12).

It is important to note that in the first commandment, "Thou shalt have no other gods before me," the word *before* is translated from the Hebrew as *in hostility toward*. Surely, if one loves Christ, one must not be hostile toward Him or His bride. Otherwise, one has committed spiritual adultery and can become separated from God.

Perhaps you know someone who used to be a member of the Seventh-day Adventist Church but has left because he or she thinks there is too much sin in the church, or the leadership is corrupted, or the church is refusing additional light, or God is no longer with the church, or we are the remnant of the remnant. Whoever the person, or whatever the reasons given, you will generally detect a strain of hostility toward the so-called apostate corporate church. It is interesting, therefore, that in the first commandment God orders us not to have any gods of hostility toward Him. In light of this, consider a statement in the Spirit of Prophecy: "I warn the Seventh-day Adventist Church to be careful how you receive every new notion and those who claim to have great light. The character of their work seems to be to accuse and to tear down" (*Selected Messages,* book 2, p. 69).

What is your attitude toward the bride? Do not let some personal disagreement or hurt feeling sever your connection to the body. Ask Jesus for healing; He can provide it.

Listen, friends; these stories are nothing new. Read Joshua chapter 7 where God ordered the whole household of Achan to be stoned, killed, and burned over a seemingly trivial thing. No matter how trivial it may seem, it still comes down to the disobedience of God's commands, and that is what makes it a major error.

How, then, are the separated ones not keeping God's commandments? Let us go back to the *self* and *I,* mentioned earlier. They have become their own gods of hostility and have committed spiritual adultery and separated themselves.

The circumstances surrounding the separation of Paul and Barnabas by the Holy Spirit shows there is a definite line of service for each individual. Clearly, the Lord works through His appointed agencies in His organized church. Just because we do not see eye to eye with someone does not mean we should separate from the body; Paul and

Barnabas did not.

God has made His church on earth a channel of light, and through it He communicates His purposes and His will. He does not give a single one of His servants an experience independent or contrary to the church's teachings on Scripture. Neither does He give one person knowledge of His will for the entire church while the church, Christ's body, is left in the dark.

Ellen White makes it easy to understand in that the Seventh-day Adventist Church has been chosen by God to be an ambassador for Him in the last work of salvation. Do you know what the word *last* means? The Seventh-day Adventist Church will do the *last* work of salvation. "God has bestowed the highest power under heaven upon His church. It is the voice of God in His united people in church capacity which is to be respected" (*Testimonies for the Church*, vol. 3, p. 451). Be sensible, friends, and read the context. Ellen is not talking about the Catholics, Jews, Protestants, or any other religious group; she is speaking of the Seventh-day Adventist Church.

Listen to the passages in the *Testimonies for the Church* that speak about the close of probation and the shaking among God's people, and you will see that a purer, holier people will arise. "The Lord has not given you a message to call the Seventh-day Adventists Babylon, and to call the people of God to come out of her. All the reasons you may present cannot have weight with me on this subject, because the Lord has given me decided light that is opposed to such a message" (*Selected Messages*, book 2, p. 63).

> Again I say, The Lord has not spoken by any messenger who calls the church that keeps the commandments of God, Babylon.... I know that the Lord loves His church. It is not to be disorganized or broken up into independent atoms. There is not the least consistency

in this; there is not the least evidence that such a thing will be. Those who shall heed this false message and try to leaven others will be deceived and prepared to receive advanced delusions, and they will come to nought.... I warn the Seventh- day Adventist Church to be careful how you receive every new notion and those who claim to have great light. The character of their work seems to be to accuse and to tear down. (*Selected Messages*, book 2, pp. 68, 69)

Ponder also the following revelations: "Some have advanced the thought that as we near the close of time, every child of God will act independently of any religious organization. But I have been instructed by the Lord that in this work there is no such thing as every man's being independent" (*Testimonies for the Church*, vol. 9, p. 258).

I tell you my brothers and sisters, the Lord *has* an organized body through whom He will work. When anyone is drawing apart from the organized body of God's commandment-keeping people, when he begins to weigh the church in his human scales and begins to pronounce judgment against him, *then* you may *know* that *God is not leading him.* He is on the wrong track! (*Selected Messages*, book 3, p. 18, 19, italics mine)

How much clearer does it have to be, my friends? One cannot truly love Jesus intimately if one is not married to Him. One is not married to Him unless one is His bride. Remember His bride is His people, the church. It is crystal clear that God makes His testimonies known through the Seventh-day Adventist Church. Even Satan knows the Word of God to be genuine, and he is working to deceive each one of us. One of Satan's last deceptions is to make the testimonies of no effect. The Bible identifies the last true remnant church organization to be the Seventh-day Adventist Church. Now, if you do not believe what you are reading, or if you are one of those who turn away from this truth at this time, then prepare yourself for advanced delusions.

Now, listen carefully. There are many of God's people who are not members of the Seventh-day Adventist Church organized body but who are still part of the body of Christ, because they are faithfully living a life of commitment to God in their knowledge of truth. It may be that they will be "called out" to join the organized body, or God may choose to keep them where they are as a witness for Him for a special purpose. Whatever the case, all the faithful of any denomination can be a part of the body of Christ. By the same token, many who belong to the organized Seventh-day Adventist Church may not be members of the body of Christ because they are continuously unfaithful and apostate.

What do you really think of God with respect to His power and authority over His church? Do you think He is in control? Take the *p* from *power* and you have *ower (our)*. Take the *ity* from *authority* and you have *author*. In God's power and authority over His church, He is our Author. Away from His power and authority all you have left is PITY, and it honestly becomes a pitiful situation when we try to limit God to our own mentality.

If He is not in command, we are not subject to Him. If God is in agreement with what the Bible states, He is in control. It is impossible for anyone to limit God to their own mindset. Do you truly believe the Word of God? "There is no need to doubt, to be fearful that the work will not succeed. God is at the head of the work, and He will set everything in order. If matters need adjusting at the head of the work, God will attend to that and work to right every wrong. Let us have faith that God is going to carry the noble ship which bears the people of God safely into port" (*Selected Messages*, book 2, p. 390).

Understand that there has always been an apostasy in the church from the time in the Garden of Eden to this day. But understand also, there is a reason for this betrayal. "God has permitted apostasies to take place in order to show how little dependence can be placed in man. We are always to look to God; His word is not Yea and Nay, but Yea and Amen" (*Selected Messages*, book 2, p. 395).

Please reconsider your position with God; confess your rebellion, repent of your sins and let God do His work. Do not try to do His work for Him. Jesus did not call us his vicars. He called us His witnesses. Are we witnessing or "vicaring"?

We are sorry there are defective members, that there are tares amid the wheat. Evils exist in the church and will until the end of the world (did you get that?). The church in these last days is to be the light of the world, which is polluted and demoralized by sin. The Seventh-day Adventist Church, enfeebled and defective, needing to be reproved, warned, and counseled, "is the only object upon earth upon which Christ bestows His supreme regard" (*Testimonies to Ministers*, p. 49).

Following are a few of Ellen White's statements testifying to the firm and divine foundation of the Seventh-day Adventist Church.

"I am instructed to say to Seventh-day Adventists the world over, God has called us as a people to be a peculiar treasure unto Himself. He has appointed that His church on earth shall stand perfectly united in the Spirit and counsel of the Lord of hosts to the end of time" (*Selected Messages*, book 2, p. 397). Do you understand that? The end of time!

"We cannot now step off the foundation that God has established. We cannot now enter into any new organization; for this would mean apostasy from the truth" (*Selected Messages*, book 2, p. 390).

Apostasy? Unfaithful to God? Can you keep the commandments in apostasy? It is true, "The church has sadly failed to meet the expectations of her redeemer, and yet the Lord does not withdraw Himself from His people" (*Signs of the Times*, November 13, 1901).

Let us be careful when we talk about apostasy. Apostasy means to forsake or abandon. Yes, many within the church have forsaken and abandoned what they once professed or adhered to as the truth. And some of these people are still listed as members in their local church. This lack of adherence needs to be addressed. This matter needs attention. However, the church has not turned its back on God; it still adheres to the same fundamental truths. Yes, it is those who leave and disassociate themselves from the main, corporate church who commit an apostasy, whatever they call themselves Reform Seventh-day Adventists or the like. The bottom line is apostasy. How are you classified?

"We are Seventh-day Adventists. Are we ashamed of our name? We answer, 'No, no! We are not. It is the name the Lord has given us. It points out the truth that is to be the test of the churches'" (*Selected Messages*, book 2, p. 384).

"We are Seventh-day Adventists and of this name we are never to be ashamed. As a people we must take a firm stand for truth and righteousness. Thus we shall glorify God. We are to be delivered from dangers, not ensnared and corrupted by them. That this may be, we must look ever to Jesus, the Author and Finisher of our faith" (*Selected Messages*, book 2, p. 384).

So as it is written, so let it be done. "God has invested His church with special authority and power, which no one can be justified in disregarding and despising; for he who does this despises the voice of God" (*Gospel Workers*, p. 444).

At the age of thirty-three Jesus was condemned to the death penalty. At that time crucifixion was the worst death to endure. Only the worst criminals were condemned to be crucified. Yet it was even more dreadful for Jesus, for unlike other criminals condemned to death by crucifixion, Jesus was nailed to the cross by His hands and feet rather than tied. Each nail was six to eight inches long. The nails were driven into His wrists—not into His palms as is commonly portrayed. There is a tendon in the wrist that extends to the shoulder. The Roman guards knew that when the nails were hammered into the wrist the tendon would tear and break, forcing Jesus to use His back muscles to support Himself so that He could breathe.

Both of His feet were nailed together. Thus He was forced to support Himself on the single nail that impaled His feet to the cross. Jesus could not support Himself with His legs for long because of the pain, so He was forced to alternate between arching His back and using His legs just to continue to breath. Imagine the struggle, the pain, the suffering, the courage.

Jesus endured this reality for more than three hours. Yes, more than three hours! Can you imagine this kind of suffering? A few minutes before He died, Jesus stopped bleeding. Instead, water flowed from His wounds, and not just the wounds to His hands and feet and His side. He had many more wounds all over His body. Before being nailed to the cross, Jesus was whipped and beaten. The whipping was so severe that it tore the flesh from His body. The beating so horrific that His face was torn and His beard ripped from His face in places. The crown of thorns (two to three inch thorns) cut deeply into His scalp. Most men would not have survived this torture. He had no more blood to bleed out—only water poured from His wounds. The human adult body contains about 3.5 liters (just less than a gallon) of blood. Because water poured out of Jesus' body, it is assumed that He lost all of His blood on the cross.

He suffered all of this in addition to the humiliation He endured after carrying His own cross for almost two kilometers while the crowd spat in His face and threw rocks at Him. Jesus had to endure this experience so that we may have free access to God and that our sins can be washed away. Don't ignore this. Jesus Christ died for you! Accept the reality, the truth, that Jesus is the only salvation for the world. Take a moment to appreciate the power of God in your life as you do what pleases Him. He said, "Whoever acknowledges me before men, I will also acknowledge him before my Father in heaven. But whoever disowns me before men, I will disown him before my Father in heaven" (Matt. 10:32, 33, NIV).

# Chapter Two

# Advanced Delusions

*Even Him, whose coming is after the working of Satan with all power and signs and lying wonders, and with all deceivableness of unrighteousness in them that perish; because they receive not the love of the truth, that they might be saved. And for this cause, God shall send them strong delusion, that they should believe a lie—2 Thess. 2:9–11.*

Can you have the truth and not love it? Is it the love of the truth that one must have in order to be saved? The Scriptures tell us that Jesus is "the way, the truth and the life" (John 14:6). Jesus saves, but can He save the one who does not love Him? So if we love the truth and we love Him, does He give us life (salvation)?

Now get this, because it is very important. If we love Jesus, who is the truth, we must love everything He represents, especially that upon which He "bestows His supreme regard." Does that ring a bell? Upon what does He bestow His supreme regard? The answer is His church because it is His bride. So it is only natural for a man to bestow his highest regard upon the one woman he loves. This is how God feels about *His* bride, the church. Therefore, you would think that His bride would love God as much as He loves her. Unfortunately, the church does not love God as much as He loves her, at least not yet. Fortunately, she will love Him in the last days just before the return of Jesus. This love will be developed because of many reasons, including a knowledge of the truth, persecution, commitment, compassion and a love for the truth.

**Pause now:** Take your Bible and read Revelation 3:14–22.

In this passage of Revelation, we find a deplorable attitude in His bride. She will eventually overcome through persecution during the latter rain of the Holy Spirit and become the kind of woman she ought to be, pure! However, it is because of the lack of love for the truth that God sends a strong delusion so that those who do not love the truth shall believe a lie.

Now, we must admit that in every Christian religion, there is some truth. However, it is not just the "some truth" that is the issue here. It is every truth that God reveals to us that makes the difference and becomes the issue. If we are not willing to love Him enough to accept all the truth He presents, then we are, in effect, rejecting truth—and Jesus. Without the experience of love for the truth, we will believe lies and not recognize truth, and in reality, Jesus is rejected.

Jesus reveals what will happen in the hearts of many as earth's history draws to a close. "And then [in the last days] shall many be offended and shall betray one another and shall hate one another; and many false prophets shall rise and shall deceive many. And because iniquity shall abound, the love of many shall wax cold" (Matt. 24:10–12). Here Jesus is warning us, before it happens, that many will be offended. Their love will grow cold, and they will leave the faith. When someone leaves the church, do we not say that they have left the faith? Therefore, leaving the church is stepping off the foundation, an apostasy from the truth." Remember Ellen White's counsel mentioned in Chapter One of this book, out of *Selected Messages*, Book 2, page 390: "We cannot now step off the foundation that God has established. We cannot now enter into any new organization; for this would mean apostasy from the truth."

Consider the following Bible texts:

"Thou art my rock and my fortress" (Psalm 31:3).

"Upon this rock I will build my church" (Matt. 16:18).

"But Christ as a son over his own house; whose house are we…" (Heb. 3:6).

"…the church, which is his body…" (Eph. 1:22, 23).

The Scriptures are clear; Jesus is the rock or foundation upon which His church (faithful humans) is built. The foundation and the church becomes one unit. Any part that is separated from the structure becomes apostate.

The following metaphors found in the verses above are all synonyms for the church: the bride, the faith, whose house we are, and the body. Notice what happens when one turns away from these. Five things take place as recorded in Matthew 24:10–12:

1.  They betray each other (expose).
2.  Many false prophets arise (lies).
3.  Many are deceived (tricked).
4.  Love grows cold (no compassion).
5.  They hate each other (hostility).

Also, we must include in this list those who believe that Christ cannot manage or control His church properly. They take it upon themselves to do His work, thinking they are the ones being led by the Holy Spirit. When they fail to follow the precepts God has set forth, great damage is done.

Now ask yourself this question, what is the attitude toward the body? In essence, the departed ones think that God cannot control things. This belief appears to be one of accusation and of tearing down, thus classifying them with Matthew 24:10–12. Understand something else here. Some of those who leave the faith or the church are not necessarily absent from it; in other words, their departure is spiritual, not physical. Their presence becomes a type of wolf–among-sheep scenario. This, too, contributes to the fulfillment of Matthew 24:10–12.

Now let us consider this: never before in history of modern times have we seen such an influx of false prophets. Jesus warns: "Watch out for false prophets, they come to you in sheep's clothes, but inwardly they are ferocious wolves. By their fruits you will know them" (Matt. 7:15, 16, RV). False prophets are liars, and the only way to expose a liar is to know the truth. Remember, Satan has a counterfeit for every truth, and if it were possible, to deceive even the very elect. Therefore, the very elect must know the truth and what fruits are produced by the deceiver. In order to recognize a false prophet, one must also recognize the fruits of the True One.

Notice something else; the most effective false prophet is one who is in the truth (not of the truth), the wolf in sheep's clothing, the insider, and the undercover agent. Satan and his demons recognize the tremendous benefits of this system and the effectiveness of promoting false teachings and real deceptions derived from partial truths. Indeed, Satan has infiltrated the truth with strong delusions.

If you are a Seventh-day Adventist, and you hear about an individual who is receiving revelations from God and inquire as to the message he or she bears, would you not find the revelation more impressive if you discovered the person was a Seventh-day Adventist instead of a Catholic or Baptist or follower of any other religion? You may be more likely to accept his or her message without a thorough investigation into the truth.

Recognizing a false prophet (accuser, liar, and criticizer) can be very difficult at times. One reason why Satan's plan is so effective is that he knows the true Word of God. He specializes in mixing error with truth. We can be sure that some of our supposed brothers or sisters who have been in the truth for years are doing the work of the devil. Do not forget the wolf, my friend.

Are you beginning to recognize that a prophet does not have to be one who receives visions or dreams directly from God? A true prophet is not just someone who discloses divine revelations from God or is able to foretell the future. A prophet can also be a spokesperson, an advocate, one who supports and defends a cause. Does this ring any bells? Maybe we have more false prophets around than we thought!

Recall Ephesians 4:11: "And he gave some, apostles; and some, prophets; and some, evangelists; and some, pastors and teachers." Notice that the *apostles, prophets, evangelists, pastors,* and *teachers* are plural. Also, it is all for the building up of the church, for knowledge of the truth and for unity, perfection, and spiritual growth into the fullness of Christ. We are not E. G. White–type prophets, but we can easily be the advocate-type prophet, teacher, evangelist, or pastor. (And speaking of pastors, 1 Peter 2:9 states about all believers, "you are a royal priesthood.") Furthermore, verse 15 is the strongest marker of a true advocate, "speaking the truth in love."

Let's break down the apostle Paul's description of a false prophet's method to mislead unassuming, ungrounded souls: "That we henceforth be no more children [spiritually immature], tossed to and fro, and carried about with every wind of doctrine [false teachings], by the sleight of men, [tricks and skills], and cunning craftiness [shrewd and experienced] whereby they lie and wait to deceive [fool you]" (Eph. 4:14). Now, if that does not sound like a false prophet (advocate), then what does?

Now, let us recognize that God has given a genuine channel of light through Ellen White. Therefore, it stands to reason that Satan will have his people on the scene. Christ came and warned us of Satan's deception. "For there shall arise false Christs, and false prophets" (Matt. 24:24). Do not be deceived, cheated, or misled in Lucifer's direction. Before you can have a false anything you must first have the true."

The Bible instructs us to identify the truth in three basic ways. No matter who does the trickery, we can recognize a false prophet if we can identify the truth. By the law, testimony and the fruits of their labor, we will identify the prophet.

*The law*, of course, is the Ten Commandments. If one does not teach and live in harmony with all Ten Commandments or belittles the law in any consistent manner through disobedience or misrepresentation, beware!

*The testimony* is the entire scriptural revelation given to humankind by God. If everything one teaches is not in complete harmony with the Scriptures, beware! "To the law and to the testimony: if they speak not according to this word, it is because there is no light in them" (Isa. 8:20).

*The fruits* are characteristics by which we recognize an individual's distinctive qualities, traits, or moral excellence. It is like a certificate of their conduct or ability. And, so just as an apple comes from an apple tree, a true prophet of God will portray the true eminence of God. The "fruit of Spirit is love, joy, peace, patience, kindness, goodness, faithfulness, gentleness and self–control" (Gal. 5:22, 23, NIV).

Remember that we are talking 100 percent, not 99 percent participation. If they do not adhere to the whole law, if they do not teach completely in line with the truth of the Scriptures, if they change one jot (dot) or tittle (crossing of the *t*), and if they do not portray the characteristics of God in their lives, beware!

One word of caution at this point; let us leave a little room for human error, OK? "For all have sinned, and come short of the glory of God" (Rom. 3:23). However, "For of this you can be sure: No immoral, impure or greedy person—such a man as an idolater—has any inheritance in the kingdom of Christ and of God. Let no one deceive you with empty words, for because of such things God's wrath comes on those who are disobedient. Therefore do not be partners with them"

(Eph. 5:5–7, NIV). Being in the truth is one thing, but being of the truth is altogether different. That is the proof of the pudding.

Have you ever met anyone who believes his own lies? The logical reaction would be to say: Wow, this person is something else. How deluded can he be? Believing his own lies is about as far as a liar can go!

Can we not say, then, this person is advanced? You need to come to the realization, dear friend, that those who are in the truth and not of the truth can believe the deception of their own lies. The only real antidote is to receive the love of the truth. But how, you ask, can we be deluded to believe these lies? Answer: by not being willing to let the Holy Spirit work in our minds to help create an unselfish attitude! Have you ever met an unselfish liar? Unless one not only is grounded and rooted in the truth but also loves the truth, the Bible says that God will allow that person to receive strong delusions and believe lies.

Catch this now: when one *is not* in the truth and believes lies, one is deluded. But, when one *is in* the truth and believes lies, one is receiving advanced delusions.

Now, let us put this puzzle together. To review, the Bible says that God is truth and God is love. God's body is His church, and we have already clearly identified His church. Therefore, if one does not have the love of the truth, that individual, in effect, does not love God, His body, or His church. You cannot hate His people and love Him. You cannot hate His body and love Him. You cannot separate yourself from His church body for any reason and simultaneously say you love God. In essence, Jesus said it's all or nothing. We must accept God and all that He has ordained, or we accept none of it. That is the bottom line, my friend.

Listen now. Jesus has two bodies, His physical flesh body and His spiritual church body, which contains physical flesh-and-blood people. Look what happened to His flesh body! When He was entering into His time of trouble and great tribulation, just before the cross, His body was bruised, battered, torn, bleeding, and almost beyond recognition. His face was so changed by the anguish that His own disciples hardly recognized Him in body at Gethsemane.

Now, consider His church body today as it is entering into the time of trouble and great tribulation. Satan has (with the help of many humans) taken the body of Christ (spiritual church) and battered, bruised, and torn it apart, and it is bleeding. Many of its disciples struggle to recognize the sabotage. Unfortunately, some will leave the church to their own destruction as Judas did. Yet some will deny as Peter did. But praise God, some will be found at the foot of the cross, as Mary Magdalene was, with an unquenchable thirst for Christ, their Savior. Mary recognized His person, and nothing separated her or prevented her from being there until the end of His suffering on the cross.

Yes, it is the love for Christ and His body (church) that is the bonding agent that glues His people fast to the oneness of God. And when the winds of false doctrine blow, or the delusions of deceit push against the true remnant church, when the cares of this life surround them, the church will stand true because the love of the truth will keep her standing. Jesus promises, "But he that shall endure unto the end, the same shall be saved" (Matt. 24:13).

Mary Magdalene was in love with Christ, and she stayed. Peter loved Christ, but selfishness separated him from Jesus. After much agony, Peter realized his mistake and put self aside, fell in love with Jesus, and was forgiven. He came back to the truth! My friend, if you cannot be quite like Mary, please do not be like Judas. Return to God like Peter and love the truth in the fullness and stature of Christ.

As the early Christians awaited the outpouring of the Holy Spirit, they moved toward closer unity, putting away all differences and all desires for supremacy. If we would study Christ instead of each other, it would elevate our thoughts, purify our minds, transform our characters, and we would reflect His kind of love. Truly, we will have the love for the truth, and it will classify us with Jesus.

Two friends were walking
Through the desert.
During some point of the
Journey, they had an
Argument; and one friend
Slapped the other one
In the face.

The one who got slapped
Was hurt, but without
Saying anything,
Wrote this in the sand,
"Today my best friend
Slapped me in the face."

They kept on walking
Until they found an oasis
Where they decided
To take a bath.

The one who had been
Slapped got stuck in the
Mire and started drowning,
But the friend saved him.

After he recovered from
The near drowning,
He wrote on a stone,
"Today my best friend
Saved my life."

The friend who had slapped
And saved his best friend
Asked him, "After I hurt you,
You wrote in the sand, and now
You write on a stone. Why?"

The friend replied,
"When someone hurts us,
We should write it down
In sand, where winds of
Forgiveness can erase it."

"But when someone does something good for us,
We must engrave it in stone
Where no wind can ever erase it."

Learn to write
Your hurts in
The sand and to
Carve your
Benefits in stone.

# Classified

They say it takes a
Minute to find a special person,
An hour to appreciate them,
A day to love them,
But then, an entire life to forget them.

Do not value the things
You have in your life, but value
*Who* you have known in your life!

# Chapter Three

# **Elevators**

Learn a parable of an Eagle. WHAT IF the Eagle has one of the longest life spans among birds. WHAT IF it can live up to seventy years, but to reach this age, the eagle must make a hard decision. In its 40s its long and flexible talons can no longer grab its prey. Its long and sharp beak becomes bent. Its heavy wings and thick feathers become stuck to its chest, making it difficult to fly. WHAT IF the eagle is left with only two options: die or go through a painful process of change that lasts about 150 days.

WHAT IF this process requires that the eagle fly to a mountain top and sit on its nest. There the eagle knocks its beak against a rock until it is plucked out. After plucking it out, the eagle has to wait for a new beak to grow back, and then it begins plucking out its talons. When its new talons grow back, the eagle then begins plucking its feathers out. Then WHAT IF after five long months the eagle takes its famous flight of rebirth and lives for thirty or so more years.

Why is this change needed? Many times in order to survive we have to change. We sometimes need to get rid of old memories, habits, and other past traditions. Freed from past burdens, we can take advantage of the present.

When it rains most birds head for shelter. WHAT IF the Eagle is the only bird that in order to avoid the rain starts flying above the clouds. When the stormy clouds of life close in on you, ask God to help you rise above the clouds to where the Son shines and classify yourself as an eagle so you can have new life in Jesus. God wants you to spread your wings and soar like the eagles.

"But they that wait upon the Lord shall renew their strength; they shall mount up with wings as eagles; they shall run, and not be weary; and they shall walk, and not faint" (Isa. 40:31).

Similar to the eagle that must weather the storms, we experience storms in this life. There certainly are ups and downs in the Christian experience. Oftentimes we are in the right elevator but get off on the wrong floor. Maybe you can relate to that. Perhaps this can be compared to the church you attend. You believe that you are in the right elevator (in the right church), but when the door slides open and you look out to see what is on that floor level, you begin to realize the floor looks different from what you conceived it to be, and you feel you might be on the wrong floor.

The first question that might come to mind is, what happened to my concept? You look around and wonder what to do. The operator says that you are on the right floor. You gasp with awe at the variety available to you, and the operator asks, "What are you looking for?" "Take me to another floor," you reply. And so up or down you go.

Let us pause in our story right here and plug in some representations. Let us say the person in the elevator is you; the elevator is the Holy Spirit, who takes you where you are directed to go; the operator is Jesus; the variety is the people; and the floor represents where to find the right robe. Now, back to the story.

"What is it that you are seeking," the operator asks. "I can help you find what you need," he continues. "Let us return to the right floor."

As you look around, you realize there are many things you did not expect to see. You thought that it was exclusive to only certain items because that is what all your studying portrayed. Your lips start quivering as you stutter the words "I-a-I-I-I was told I could find a new robe on this floor. But there are so many obstacles, so many different things and scores of unique merchandise; there is such variety. How can you find the right robe among all these options?"

A voice whispers softly and gently in the background. It is Christ saying: "I know the way. Take my hand, follow me, and watch only me; I will lead you there. You must be sure not to let go of my hand, and keep your eyes on me at all times or you may get pushed aside by other distractions." As you follow Him, you suddenly realize He has already placed upon you the robe you needed—His robe of righteousness.

While we see many people genuinely giving their lives to Jesus and wanting to follow Him, the enemy has an abundance of ways to turn people's eyes away from the truth of Christ. Vulnerable to his attacks, we can become cold, uncomfortable, naked, and miserable; the robe falls. Then reality hits, and we recognize that the excitement of the first love has faded into disappointment.

Oh, how important it is that we keep our eyes fixed on the right one. Jesus said, "And I, if I be lifted up from the earth, will draw all men unto me" (John 12:32). Too often we take our eyes off Jesus, get confused, and become caught up in the elevator encounter. So up and down we go, eyes become dim, and we do not recognize the one who is leading us.

Jesus wants to lift us up with the elevator. He wants to help us find the robe, the white garment so necessary for our salvation. Oh, how wretched, miserable, poor, blind, and naked we become when we take our eyes off Jesus. We need eye salve to help us see more clearly. Read Revelation 3:14–22 and pray for understanding. Jesus Himself recognizes that we are wretched, miserable, poor, blind, and naked, yet He does not at once reject us, but offers a way back to Him. Only those individuals who continue to refuse to be led by Him will be spewed out.

Yes, yes, yes, in many instances the condition of the church is deplorable. Remember, however, the church is an association of leaders and laypersons, and every faithful one is part of the church body.

There are many who act surprised to see all the sins in the church and think God cannot handle it. Furthermore, they try to do His work for Him by taking matters into their own hands. In reality, these people are the ones who cannot handle all the sins. Consequently, they become unhappy and confused and they separate from the truth, sometimes without even realizing it.

Being miserable and wretched is a state of mind. It is a mental attitude called unhappiness, a lack of joy. Why are people discontented? It is because they have taken their eyes off Jesus and are looking at all the distractions. When you take your eyes off Jesus, the discouragements will blind you. Instead of experiencing the joy of your Lord, you submit yourself to sorrow.

Discouragements can blind one to the understanding that God's love is steadfast. No matter what, He is still there reaching out, waiting for us to once again take His hand. The kind of blindness one receives from opposition is the inability to properly discern spiritual things. The cure for that is the eye salve of the Holy Spirit. Without Him, we cannot see spiritual things clearly or experience the joy of the Lord.

Without the Holy Spirit in our lives, we become spiritually poor. Jesus says, "Buy of me gold tried in the fire" (Rev. 3:18). The gold tried in fire is faith that works by love. It is through the power of the Holy Spirit eye salve that one can spiritually discern things and receive the faith that works by, and through, love, thus making us spiritually rich. It enables us to have the white robe of Christ's righteousness that we may be clothed and have our nakedness, or sinfulness, covered.

Do you get the picture? We have a decision to make as to whether or not we want the Holy Spirit experience, the white robe. We need to understand four things.

1.  The condition of the church is intensely distasteful, and God

knows it: "I know thy works.... knowest not that thou art wretched, and miserable, and poor, and blind, and naked" (Rev. 3:15, 17).

2. God (not humanity) has the antidote or solution. "I counsel thee to buy of me gold tried in the fire, that thou mayest be rich; and white raiment, that thou mayest be clothed, and that the shame of thy nakedness do not appear; and anoint thine eyes with eyesalve, that thou mayest see. As many as I love, I rebuke and chasten: be zealous therefore, and repent" (Rev. 3:18, 19).

3. God gives us the invitation. "Behold, I stand at the door, and knock; if any man hear my voice and open the door, I will come in to him and will sup with him, and he with me" (Rev. 3:20).

4. If we accept the invitation, He will restore us. "To him that overcometh will I grant to sit with me in my throne, even as I also overcame, and am set down with My Father in his throne" (Rev. 3:21).

Nobody can understand his or her own errors apart from God's insight. "The heart is deceitful above all things, and desperately wicked: who can know it?" (Jer. 17:9). The Spirit of Prophecy corroborates the Bible's assessment of the human heart:

> The lips may express a poverty of soul that the heart does not acknowledge. While speaking to God of poverty of spirit, the heart may be swelling with the conceit of its own superior humility and exalted righteousness. In one way only can a true knowledge of self be obtained. We must behold Christ. It is ignorance of Him that makes men so uplifted in their own righteousness. When we contemplate His purity and excellence, we

shall see our own weakness, poverty and defects as they really are. We shall see ourselves lost and hopeless, clad in garments of self-righteousness like every other sinner. We shall see that if we are ever saved, it will not be through our own goodness, but through God's infinite grace. (*Christ's Object Lessons*, p. 159)

Let us run to Him who knows us, redeemed us, and can save us from all of the wayfaring tendencies that can easily ensnare us.

Let us talk about another kind of elevator, and let's use our imagination. Let's say we can only go up in this type of elevator; it is called an uplift. None of these uplifts will ever take you down. One such uplift is called praise. Read how it worked for David:

Because your love is better than life, my lips will glorify you. I will praise you as long as I live, and in your name I will lift up my hands. My soul will be satisfied, as with the richest of foods, with singing lips my mouth will praise you. On my bed I remember you; I think of you through the watches of the night. Because you are my help, I sing in the shadow of your wings. My soul clings to you; your right hand upholds me. (Ps. 63:3–8, NIV).

David dedicated his entire day and night to praising God any way he could, and as verse 8 states, God rewarded him by upholding, or uplifting, him.

Another uplift elevator can be identified as humility. "Humble yourselves in the sight of the Lord and he shall lift you up" (James 4:10). True humility is submissiveness. When we submit ourselves to God, we are willing to follow Him wherever He leads, and He promises to lift us up. "Humble yourselves therefore under the mighty hand of

God, that he may exalt you in due time" (1 Pet. 5:6). If we truly humble ourselves before God and acknowledge all He is and has done for us, we will recognize His grace toward us and want to praise Him always. How time-consuming, how uplifting, how rewarding!

Listen, friend:

> The end of all things is near. Therefore be clear minded and self-controlled so that you can pray. Above all, love each other deeply, because love covers over a multitude of sins. Offer hospitality to one another without grumbling. Each one should use whatever gift he has received to serve others, faithfully administering God's grace in its various forms. If anyone speaks, he should do it as one speaking the very words of God. If anyone serves, he should do it with the strength God provides, so that in all things God may be praised through Jesus Christ. To him be the glory and power forever and ever. Amen. (1 Pet. 4:7-11, NIV)

We began this chapter with the example of the eagle, and we are ending this chapter with another example from nature. If you put a buzzard in a pen that is six feet by eight feet by six feet deep and is open at the top, the bird, in spite of its ability to fly, will be an absolute prisoner. A buzzard always begins flying from the ground with a take-off run of ten to twelve feet. Without space to run, as is its habit, it will not even attempt to fly but will remain a prisoner for life in a small jail with no top.

The ordinary bat that flies at night is a remarkable creature in the air. However, the bat cannot takeoff from a flat level surface. If it is placed on one all it can do is shuffle around helplessly and no doubt painfully until it reaches some slight elevation from which it can throw itself into the air. Then at once it takes off in a flash.

A bumblebee, if put into an open glass will be there until it dies unless it is taken out. It never sees the means of escape at the top but persists in trying to find some way out through the sides near the bottom of the glass. It will seek a way of escape where non exists until it completely destroys itself.

In many ways people are like the buzzard, the bat, and the bumblebee. We struggle with all our problems and frustrations, never realizing that all we have to do is change our position or look up. That's the answer. The escape route from earth and the solution to our problems is to simply look to Jesus our Savior. JUST LOOK UP!

Sorrow looks back, worry looks around, but faith looks up.

Live simply, love generously, care deeply, speak kindly, and trust in the Creator Jesus Christ who loves you. Do you want to be classified with those who are going up or going down?

# Chapter Four

# Scrawny Wheat and Healthy Tares

Sam groaned, "There, it is finally done," as he planted the last bean seed in his garden. "Now, all I have to do is keep it watered, and soon the plants will appear."

Several days later he noticed little green shoots coming up all over his garden. "Wow!" he exclaimed. "My garden is growing." Sam was only twelve years old, and it was his first garden, and it was healthy looking. Green plants were coming up all over the tilled ground. His father asked, "Where did you put the string beans?" Sam answered, "Over there, right next to the radishes." His father looked over to where Sam was pointing and saw a big patch of little green plants shooting up out of the soil in an incredibly irregular manner.

Sam's father told Sam that he was supposed to plant the seeds in even rows and put markers at the end of the rows so that the plants could be identified. But Sam failed to do the one exceptionally important thing, to distinguish the different types of seeds that were planted by putting them in rows and marking them. It was important to be able to identify the plants when it came time for harvest.

One week later Sam went out to hoe his garden and discovered that he could not tell the difference between the good plants and the weeds.

Matthew 13:24, 25 is an example of what happened to Sam. "The kingdom of heaven is likened unto a man which sowed good seed in his field: But while men slept, his enemy came and sowed tares among the wheat, and went his way." What could Sam do? The plants looked the same. If He started pulling up what he thought might be weeds, then he might also pluck up the good plants.

The only thing that Sam could do was to let the plants mature until he could tell the difference between the good and bad ones by identifying the different types of fruit. Unfortunately, when good seeds are planted among weeds, the tares crowd out the wheat from the sunlight. Similarly, the tares rob the good plants of nutrients. During this process, the tares get entangled with the wheat both above the ground and all the way down into the root system. Therefore, it becomes dreadfully difficult to pull the tares without either seriously damaging or killing the wheat. It seems at this point the tares are healthier than the wheat.

After Sam's garden matured enough to start weeding out the tares, his father took the time to show Sam how to remove the weeds. Very carefully and with much patience, his father pulled the tares from the garden, taking great pain not to disturb the good plants. The garden was weeded after a great deal of back-breaking work and what seemed like endless hours of time. However, because of the tares, there was a loss of good plants. It is a continual vigilant job to keep the garden cleared of weeds until harvest time.

You see, my friend, God knows the wheat from the tares as did Sam's father, and He knows how and when to remove the tares from His garden with minimal damage. Unless the wheat has its own sound root system in the ground, some of the good plants will be uprooted with the tares.

Let us analyze this for a few moments. There are a lot of things we need to understand as they relate to our Christian experience. We need to realize that God is the Gardener, and the church is the garden.

Moreover, the Holy Spirit is what keeps the garden producing the right kind of fruit.

Speaking of the Holy Spirit, John 16:13 says, "He will guide you into all truth." This is the tending of the garden. It is the angels who are the working forces for the Holy Spirit. Hebrews 1:7, 14 lets us know that they are sent forth to minister in the garden. In addition to this, the angels also help gather in the harvest. "And then shall He [Christ] send his angels, and shall gather his elect [wheat] from the four winds, from the uttermost part of the earth to the uttermost part of heaven" (Mark 13:27).

At this point in your reading, a logical question would be, When is the harvest? Maybe you have not considered that the harvest is when Jesus is coming back the second time. Furthermore, harvest could also be the end of a probationary time. Therefore, the harvest is both continual and climactic. It is continual in the sense that when one dies, one's probationary time has ended and one's eternal destiny sealed, thus determining what is either wheat or a tare. This is the continual harvest. The climactic harvest takes place when probation closes for all the living just prior to Christ's second coming. Those taken to heaven and who live are the wheat. Those left behind are the tares and are burned.

Face it; there are some of us who feel like we have been through the "mill." Maybe you are one of those who have been tossed in the wind to separate the chaff. Do you think that you have been cut down, shaken about, and shifted? Maybe you know someone who has remained true to God and loves truth so passionately that he or she has not been blown away by wind, lies, or outside influences. Millions of people fit into this classification. They have died in the Lord, so to speak, and have been laid down in storage, the grave, until the climactic harvest of the first resurrection. Where are you classified?

When Jesus returns the second time, the pure wheat will be taken into the heavenly garner (silo or storehouse). It is only the pure grain without the chaff that goes into the storehouse, and it is the angels who take in the grain.

Now, notice something again. The harvest does not begin when the grain is taken into the storehouse; this is only a phase of the harvest. Before the wheat can be collected, the stalks must be cut and the chaff removed from the grain. The stalks cannot be cut or separated until the wheat is classified or identified. The stems are cut, a separation made, and the chaff removed, and thus the purification process takes place.

Now, here is a question: can a tare become a grain of wheat? The answer to the question is most affirmatively yes. Likewise, we must allow the Holy Spirit to work in our lives to separate the sin from us just as the chaff is separated from the wheat. Some people think once a tare, always a tare, and once a grain of wheat, always a grain of wheat. However, on God's farm miracles happen and changes take place that are totally phenomenal and beyond human understanding. That is the beauty of the whole plan of redemption, the wonder of salvation, and the miracle of the new birth experience. The Holy Spirit's power creates a fresh, new beginning when a weed is transformed into a grain of wheat. Think of how a caterpillar changes to a butterfly. The Holy Spirit can cocoon us.

Once the wheat is identified, it is given time to ripen. This is the growing experience. Then a total separation arrives, when the stalk is cut and the wheat is isolated from the field. Remember, the field is the world. In other words, the born-again individual is separated from the worldly activities and practices that are contrary to a Christlike life. Once the stalk of grain has been cut, it is taken to the threshing area. Some of the wheat falls to the ground and remains in the field while being transferred to this area. How disturbing!

The next process is the removal of the chaff before the grain is gathered. The purpose of this process is to expose or classify the pure grain. Compare this with the life of the Christian. Those who are classified as wheat go through a process called sanctification, the threshing, where God removes the chaff, or sins, in their lives. This shaking exposes the pure grain or fruit that produces love, joy, peace, patience, kindness, goodness, gentleness, faithfulness, and self-control. These qualities are known as the fruit of the Holy Spirit (Gal. 5:22, 23).Yes, the fruit of the Holy Spirit is the character of God; it identifies His people. This fruit is the sweet, delicious taste of the grain. When the chaff is removed, and the character of Christ is fully exposed in one's life, the true grain will show.

However, take special note; not all the grain is taken into the storehouse. How doubly disturbing! Some of it may be crushed or mixed in with foreign matter, fall into the cracks of the threshing floor, or be shuffled off to one side. Not everyone who calls Jesus their Master will enter the kingdom of heaven (Matt. 7:21).

Just because you are a grain of wheat does not mean you are going into the storehouse. There is what I will refer to as good wheat and defective wheat, or scrawny wheat. You see, merely professing to be like Christ and having the character or mind of Christ are two different things. The wheat that goes into the storehouse is symbolized as the good wheat. The wheat that is left behind in the field or on the threshing floor is the defective, scrawny wheat. Just remember, the names that are taken out of the book of life were not tares. Our daily decisions are what determines and displays our character. Satan was the number one wheat in the courts of heaven, but he will end up in the lake of fire and will be destroyed.

There are so many responsibilities that enter into the successful life of a Christian. Yet much of Christianity today teaches salvation without obligation. Yes, salvation is a free gift from God, but it may cost you everything you have on earth to keep it.

One of the most powerful and effective methods Satan uses to destroy the wheat is by using the tares. Tares can be so misleading. They appear to be right, but they are ambiguous teachers. They look so much like the real wheat; they sound so true and seem to make sense. However, they produce a false impression of security. They rob the wheat of sunlight and water. The wheat becomes scrawny while the tares grow strong and healthy. They rob the soil of nutrition, and the wheat becomes defective. Have you ever seen a grain of wheat become sickly because it was covered from the sun (Son), or have you ever seen a defective grain from lack of proper nutrition (Bible study) and water (Holy Spirit)?

Tares also have a way of crowding out the wheat and choking it. Perhaps you may know someone who has been crowded out and choked up by the entanglement of worldly pleasures, goods, and cares, so much that they lose life (Jesus) and spiritually die.

There are tares that look so much like grains of wheat, they actually think themselves to be wheat. They seem to have an attitude like they are the cream of the crop, and so they set themselves up as judge, jury, and hangman. Therefore, they pass judgment of condemnation on the Christians they think are making the mistakes or not toeing the line.

Complacency is another form of deception that Satan uses in Christians' personal lives. Let us say that the wheat itself says, "I am increased with nutrition (goods) and have plenty of sunlight (rich) and have plenty of water (need nothing). I can survive until the harvest." Little does the plant realize it is a continuous process to receive the necessary elements to sustain life.

The Bible tells us in 2 Corinthians 6:2, "Now, is the day of salvation." Did you ever stop to realize that *now* is ever present? When Christians come to the point where they think they no longer need any more life-giving properties, they begin to die. It is only when we continuously feed from the source that we maintain life. *Now* is the most important time of your life. *Now* is continuous. Make your salvation continuous in your life.

Complacency is self-satisfaction, which, again, is Satan's substitute for the fruit of the Spirit. The one who is self-satisfied is selfish. Everything flows inward to satisfy or please self, which is just the opposite of the fruit of God streaming out to share with others in a life-giving manner. Weeds of self will take over the whole garden if left alone. This is sad but true. However, there are areas where the wheat survives under certain circumstances.

It is true that God can distinguish all the tares from the wheat, and yes, only God can read the heart, but He still uses human effort to help tend His garden. We must also remember that God is the one who does the harvesting. Too often people try to do the work of the Holy Spirit, and they start doing the wrong kind of gardening. It becomes destructive instead of constructive; thus the effort ends up in total disaster.

There are many professed Christians in the church who talk the talk but do not walk the walk. In addition, they have a worldly influence on other people in the church. Likewise, those who are truly practicing the faith and portraying the fruit of the Spirit have an effect on their fellow believers.

When the fruits of the Spirit are employed, there seems to be a bonding together in prayer, testimony, and study, thus fortifying and strengthening the wheat as they grow together, automatically crowding out the tares and shutting out the enemy

Ellen White recorded a vision she had of the harvest time, about the work of separating the tares from the wheat:

> I saw that the strong hand of the enemy is set against
> the work of God, and the help and strength of every-
> one who loves the cause of truth should be enlisted;
> great interest should be manifested by them to up-
> hold the hands of those who advocate the truth, that

by steady watchcare they may shut out the enemy. All should stand as one, united in the work. Every energy of the soul should be awake, for what is done must be done quickly. I then saw the third angel. Said my accompanying angel, "Fearful is his work. Awful is his mission. He is the angel that is to select the wheat from the tares, and seal, or bind, the wheat for the heavenly garner. (*Early Writings*, pp. 117, 118)

May Ellen White's account prompt us to cling to Christ ever firmly!

Jesus said: "If ye continue in my word, then are ye my disciples indeed; and ye shall know the truth, and the truth shall make you free" (John 8:31, 32).

It is by the words of truth that the chaff is separated from the wheat. My friend, are you living and speaking and *loving* the truth? Do not be scrawny wheat to be crowded out by healthy weeds. Join the group that is banded together with the fruits of the Spirit. Classify yourself with those who are diligent students of truth by living it and loving it.

# Chapter Five

# **Nets**

In Matthew 13:10 the disciples are asking Jesus why He speaks to the people in parables, obviously not recognizing that He is speaking also to the disciples in parables. Jesus answers by saying that it is because they do not have the knowledge of the secrets of the kingdom of heaven. Furthermore, the parables will help them to understand and to be productive in their walk with God.

To supplement this illustration, Jesus explains the parable of the sower to them. One of the secrets of the kingdom of heaven (the true church) is to hear and understand the Word. If you do not hear or read the truth, you cannot understand or know it. How can you be a healthy, productive part of something you have never read or heard? In addition, you may have been informed about God's Word, but do you have a true understanding of the Word? You cannot be a productive part of God's church without an awareness of its workings. So the secret is not only hearing or reading, but also active involvement in doing the will of God.

At this point Jesus gives three more parables to the people and the disciples to reveal the likeness of the church.

First, Matthew 13:24-30 is the parable of the wheat and the tares (which we have already discussed), in which Jesus is describing the deceitful Christians along with the genuine believers. It is important that you realize how people can be moved to consider a lie, but do not be discouraged when you see the sins of those who profess to be followers. The enemy is at work in the church (kingdom), and without the power of the Holy Spirit, we render helpless. One must realize there is a weed problem. One must allow for the tares to grow among the wheat. Do not go pulling up weeds. God will deal with it in His time, and it may be someone He works through in a special way to make chastisements and also help to preserve the wheat. Remember, it is God who bundles and burns.

Second, in the parable of the mustard seeds of Matthew 13:31, 32, Jesus is saying that His church (kingdom) will start out small and become great so that all who seek Christ can find Him. Moreover, a true believer can start out small in faith and grow into a field of faith. Do not be deceived by the size; a kingdom can grow and draw others to it.

Third, in Matthew 13:33 Jesus makes a striking comparison of His church to yeast. Here Jesus establishes network marketing. The pyramid, or the down line, starts with a small measure and then grows into the whole lump (the world). God's program for church growth is *net*working.

In effect, Jesus says, "I am going to explain to you about the weeds just in case you did not grasp the meaning of this parable."

The one that sows the good seed is God; the tares belong to the counterfeit, Satan; the harvest is the end of the world; and the reapers are the angles of the Lord. Satan, his angles, and the tares will be burned when God destroys this earth. In other words, you reap what you sow. Paraphrased from Matthew 13:36-43, Jesus essentially says: "Then My children will shine as the sun, and so it will ever be in my Father's kingdom (earth made new). Now, if you have an ear to hear with, then hear what I am saying."

In Matthew 13:44-46, Jesus continues to say, basically: "Now, if you have not gotten it yet, let me explain it this way: The church is the kingdom of heaven, and it is like a hidden treasure. In this parable the individual has uncovered something that is more valuable than anything here in this world. He has found something that is priceless. It cost Him everything to get it, but in the end, the treasure far exceeds the sacrifices." In verses 45 and 46, is Jesus saying we should be willing to give up all we have in exchange for the kingdom of heaven? Here He uses another illustration, of the merchant and the pearl.

Here is the secret. Joining the church, or kingdom, may cost you everything that you have, but you must recognize that the value of it is greater than anything else you could ever have. Realizing this vital truth, you will be a happier and more complete person in body, spirit, and mind. What is the value of this present life compared to eternity with God?

In Matthew 13:47 Jesus begins with the seemingly frustrating thought again, as if to say: "For the last time I am going to try to help you understand what the kingdom of heaven is like. Now is the time to listen to these words I am telling you; it is important. The gospel is like throwing a net in the water and catching all kinds of fish."

Here is the mystery. The net is the good news of the gospel of Jesus Christ, and it attracts all kinds of people until the end of probation and the harvest of God's children at the second coming of Christ. The angels will separate the wicked from the righteous. Those who think that they can detach themselves from the bride (the church) may find themselves being bundled with the weeds to be burned. Read Matthew 13:48-50.

Do you get the picture? Jesus wants us to dwell on the treasures of the truth. The treasures of truth are the life of Christ, the love of God, the good news of salvation, God's forgiveness, the joy in the lord, the Christian's experience of the indwelling of the Holy Spirit, and all the truths of the Bible, not the sins of others.

There is another net. Can you guess what it is? It is Satan's fiery darts, and it is impossible to avoid them without the help of the

Master's hand. The fiery darts are mentioned in Ephesians 6:16, "Above all, taking the shield of faith, wherewith ye shall be able to quench all the fiery darts of the wicked." We clasp hold of the Master's hand by faith, and it is our faith in Him that quenches the fiery darts or arrows. Satan uses people to shoot these arrows at us and entangle us in a net of doubt so as to destroy our shield of faith. Some of these arrows are called neglect, abuse, contempt, discouragement, fret, doubt, and anything else that would weaken our faith in Jesus. Our faith in Jesus is our shield against these arrows. Hide yourself in Jesus and you will be shielded from this net.

The button for number seven on the phone pad has the letters PRS by it. We can use this as an abbreviation for prayers. You can be reminded that prayer is an important part of our defense. Also, seven is a number God uses to indicate completeness. God has given the Seventh-day Adventist Church the truth in its completeness. If you would like someone to pray for you and to know this completeness, then call the nearest Seventh-day Adventist pastor. Tell him you desire to be "re-classified" with the wheat and become part of that precious treasure. Tell him you want to understand and experience the completeness of the message God has for you. He's only a phone call and prayer away.

I have found that different types of prayer, such as traditional, personal, public, or meditational prayer, can offer many benefits. Some of the benefits include mental, physical, spiritual, and emotional improvements. Prayer can strengthen the brain and help prevent mental decline. Prayer can be measured as brain activity and has been scientifically proven to help reduce stress, lower blood pressure, boost resistance to illness and disease, neutralize harmful negative emotions, enhance the memory and mental functions, prevent dementia and Alzheimer's disease, decrease suffering and pain, and give you a healthier, happier, and longer life.

I have experienced prayer in my own life as an activator for help from above. So many times God has helped me through an experience simply because I have stayed connected with Him through prayer.

We serve a God of love, compassion, and forgiveness, and prayer can activate all this in a very personal way in our lives. Sometimes when we don't even feel like praying God is still there to help us.

For example, there was a time in my life when I was caught up in one of Satan's nets. It was the net of selfishness and disobedience, which eventually caused me to lose everything. I lost my business, home, church connection, friends, and family support. I even lost my own self-respect and ended up in a divorce. Satan's net had me so encompassed I decided to take my own life. I didn't think anyone cared, so I decided that I didn't care anymore either. But little did I know, God still cared, and so did others. The day I discovered it was the day God saved my life with a guinea pig.

There I was sitting on the edge of the bed with a revolver in my hand. The guinea pig, Grimmy, was in his house, which had only one small hole for him to go in and out of, and the hole was turned away from me so Grimmy could not see me, and I could not see him. His house was inside a larger box in which he had room to come out and play or eat. Standing on his hind legs, Grimmy could just barely touch the top of the box and see out. Now, remember, Grimmy couldn't see me from where he was.

As I lifted the gun to my head, Grimmy suddenly came running out of the little box, stood up against the side of the outer box, looked straight at me, and started barking. He caught my attention, and I lowered the revolver and told Grimmy to shut up and go back inside the box. Immediately he turned and went back inside the little box where he could not see me.

As I raised the gun again, Grimmy came running out a second time, and looking straight at me, he once again began to bark, but even louder than the first time. I told him to mind his own business, go back in his box, and leave me alone. Immediately he turned and went back into the box.

For the third time I raised the gun to my head, but before I could shoot, he was barking again as if to say, "Don't do it! Don't do it! We love you." I suddenly snapped to my senses and realized what was happening. God was using Grimmy to let me know He still loved me and wanted to help. God not only saved my life that day by using Grimmy, but He also cured me from ever wanting to do it again, and that was many, many years ago.

I didn't feel like praying when that day started, but you can believe I was on my knees afterward, thanking and praising God for what He had done for me.

Yes, my friend, prayer can be the scissors to cut your way out of Satan's net of destruction and change your classification. Use the phone line; it's toll free.

# Chapter Six

# God's Secret

The Bible says Jesus is coming again to planet earth. It describes what will happen before and after He arrives on the scene. God exposes many things about the magnificent event. Yet at the heart of all these revelations, God has a secret.

Deuteronomy 29:29 tells us, "The secret things belong unto the Lord our God; but those things which are revealed belong unto us and to our children for ever, that we may do all the words of this law." Fact number one: the Bible states that God has secrets! These secrets are known only to God until He reveals His message to His people through His prophets. The revelation will then belong to the Lord's children forever. "Surely the Lord God does nothing unless He reveals His secret to His servants the prophets" (Amos 3:7, NKJV). Did you get that? God says He will do nothing unless He first reveals it to His prophets. We call that Bible prophecy.

Here is another fact: "To every thing there is a season, and a time to every purpose under the heaven" (Eccl. 3:1). Now, understand that the word *season* here is not referring to winter, summer, spring, or fall. *Season* means appointed time. The point is that there is a chosen time for everything.

Next: "And God said let there be lights in the firmament of the heaven to divide the day from the night; and let them be for signs, and for seasons, and for days and years" (Gen. 1:14). Two of the reasons the sun, moon, and stars were made are for signs and seasons. We can predict when spring, summer, winter, and fall are approaching by look-ing for particular signs. The seasons can also have another meaning: an appointed time. The sun, moon, and stars can be used by God to show signs of things and events that are to happen at an appointed time. God created it that way as a built-in natural mechanism He could use down through the stream of time to identify specific times and events.

Let us review these facts:

1. God has secrets.
2. There is an appointed time for everything.
3. The sun, moon, and stars can be used by God as signs for ap-pointed times.

If you were to relate to one of the following, which one would you choose?

A day sleeper not knowing the light, a night walker walking in darkness, a daylighter knowing the light, or a night sleeper not know-ing darkness?

The following verse is helpful: "But of the times and the seasons brethren, ye have no need that I write unto you. For yourselves know perfectly that the day of the Lord so cometh as a thief in the night" (1 Thess. 5:1, 2). Recognize here that Paul writes this letter to help Christians understand something. He speaks of times and seasons in reference to the second coming of Christ and says there is no need to write about it because God's people are children of light (daylighters). True Christians know that the day of the Lord is going to come like a thief in the night. But God's people are not in darkness (nightwalkers); therefore, that day will not overtake them as would a burglar. It is the children of night or darkness who are overtaken.

The apostle Paul continues:

But ye, brethren, are not in darkness, that that day should overtake you as a thief. Ye are all the children of light, and the children of the day: we are not of the night, nor of darkness. Therefore let us not sleep, as do others; but let us watch and be sober. For they that sleep, sleep in the night, and they that be drunken are drunken in the night. But let us, who are of the day, be sober, putting on the breastplate of faith and love; and, for an helmet, the hope of salvation. For God hath not appointed us to wrath, but to obtain salvation by our Lord Jesus Christ. (1 Thess. 5:4-9)

Darkness is symbolic for a lack of preparation, knowledge, awareness, and understanding of the true Word. The children of light realize the times and the seasons as God reveals them. Paul gives the warning to watch, rather than sleep; be sober, not drunk; protect yourself with faith, love, and salvation. In comparison, Ephesians 6:11 states, "Put on the whole armor of God that ye may be able to stand against the wiles of the devil."

God is a God of light, which is spiritual understanding. Satan is the prince of darkness, and his followers do not understand the spiritual things of God because they love to be in the dark. Therefore, God has specific armor He wants His followers to have in order to protect themselves from the darkness of Satan. Read about it in 1 Thessalonians 6:11-18. Are you in the dark, not knowing, loving, or understanding God's program? Or are you wearing the armor? How are you classified?

We find in 2 Peter 3:10, the destruction of the heavens and earth are directly related to the thief-in-the-night. "But the day of the Lord will come as a thief in the night; in which the heavens shall pass away with a great noise, and the elements shall melt with fervent heat, the earth also and the works that are therein shall be burned up."

The wicked children of darkness perceive Christ's coming as a thief. But, the children of light know God as Deliverer and Savior. "Nevertheless we, according to His promise, look for new heavens and a new earth, wherein dwelleth righteousness" (2 Peter 3:13). His promise and admonition is found in John 3:15-21. Please read it now. Remember God has never revealed to us the exact time of the coming of Jesus. It is still His secret.

In Acts 1:6, 7, the disciples ask a question similar to the one asked in Matthew 24:3, Lord, when are you coming to restore? In Acts, Jesus replied, "It is not for you to know the times or the seasons, which the Father has put in His own power." In other words, it is His secret, not ours.

However, in Matthew 24:4 Jesus says, "Take heed that no man deceive you." He then gives an abundance of signs to look for that point toward His appointed, but secret, time. This is where creation begins to reveal its story in a dynamic way. This is where God uses what He created to specifically catch the attention of all His people and prepare them for the Father's selected time of Christ's appearing.

This is how Jesus prepares us, through study, prayer, and supplication. It enables us to recognize the words of God as we listen to the announcement that we have been waiting to hear on that great day. To those who have been classified as children of light, the Father will reveal His secret at the appointed time.

Now, take heed, my friend, when someone tells you that Jesus is coming on a certain date at a definite time. Nobody knows when Jesus is coming except God the Father. Seal in your heart and mind the words of Jesus, "But of that day and hour (exact season and time) knoweth no man, no, not the angels of heaven, but My Father, only" (Matt. 24:36).

Commit yourself to the Lord Jesus and do not dwell on the timing of His return. The Bible does not disclose exactly when Christ is coming. However, when the time comes for Christ to return, the Father Himself will announce His coming. "And, as God [the Father] spoke, the day and the hour of Jesus' coming and delivered the everlasting covenant to His people, He spoke one sentence, and then paused, while the words were rolling through the earth" (*Early Writings*, p. 285).

Have you ever asked why God keeps it a secret as to exactly when Christ is going to return? Understand that God wants us to live for Him. Therefore, we do not need to fret about the day that Jesus returns because we are already living for Him. Praise God for His grace.

Picture this, some have waited until the last minute to do something; they are in a hurry to get matters done, many things go wrong, and they forget important issues. Let us classify this group as the faithful procrastinators. They are choosing what they think is the easy way out, and they are waiting until the last minute without preparing. They have shaped a poor character in themselves.

In the religious or spiritual realm, we find some of God's people waiting until the last minute to prepare. These folks need a little more time to get ready because they have been procrastinating about getting things in order for the return of Christ. Guess what? These people will not make it to heaven because they lack the preparation so necessary for that event. On the other hand, the people who trust in Jesus and follow God's law are prepared for the Lord's return; they are groomed and ready for Christ's second coming. It does not actually matter when He arrives. Let us call these individuals the faithful preparers! Concentrate on the difference between these two groups, the faithful procrastinators and the faithful preparers. The faithful procrastinators are not prepared for Christ's coming.

"Watch ye therefore, and pray always, that ye may be accounted worthy to escape all these things that shall come to pass, and to stand before the Son of man" (Luke 21:36). The faithful preparation builds the kind of character God desires. This is the quality we take to heaven with us. Watching and praying constantly is what creates character. It is what merges us with the Lamb and makes us worthy. How shall we escape this wretched place if we neglect our salvation?

If we knew exactly when Jesus was coming back to earth, how many people would wait until the last minute to prepare themselves? You cannot build character for eternity overnight. You cannot build a loving relationship overnight and expect it to last for eternity. God wants us to have a loving and obedient character. Love requires commitment, commitment requires discipline, and discipline requires a proving time. Can this be what is meant by watching and praying?

Are you classified as a faithful preparer? Do you understand why God is keeping His secret? You have to be on guard; watch and pray as if you were getting ready to die. In order to be counted worthy and to escape deceit, you have to perpetually be ready in Jesus Christ. This is the preparation! God has giving us signs and warnings to watch for to confirm His word, and the promise of His returning. Abide in God and His Word and you will be ready for Jesus' coming because you read and knew the signs.

"Remember therefore how thou hast received and heard, and hold fast, and repent. If therefore thou shalt not watch, I will come on thee as a thief, and thou shalt not know what hour I will come upon thee" (Rev. 3:3). Focus briefly on the word *as* in this text. He comes *as* a thief, not *like* a thief. Remember that Jesus is speaking about timing, and the word *as* refers to the suddenness and unexpected time in which the thief will come. He does not use the word *like*, which means *almost*, *exactly*, or *equal to* because He is not coming quietly or secretly in the likeness or character of a thief.

"And this know, that if the goodman of the house had known what hour the thief would come, he would have watched, and not have suffered his house to be broken through. Be ye therefore ready also: for the Son of man cometh at an hour when ye think not" (Luke 12:39, 40).

Are you beginning to understand how important preparation is?

So remember, *as* means suddenly and unexpected, and *like* means *almost, exactly,* or *equal.* He will not come quietly or secretly. If Jesus were to come like a thief, this statement would support the theory of the secret rapture. However, if we read our Bibles, we know that the rapture of Jesus is coming with a roar. "For the Lord himself shall descend from heaven with a shout, with the voice of the archangel, and with the trump of God" (1 Thess. 4:16). And John tells us in Revelation 1:7 that people will be wailing (beating their breast) because of Him. Matthew 24:30 uses the following words to identify His coming: *mourn, power,* and *great glory.*

Christ is not coming *like* a thief, but rather *as* a thief. Beware to those who are not prepared. At this point in time, are you ready for God's return?

The good news is, if you are living in the darkness, you can re-classify yourself by turning the Light on in your life. Listen to me, it is critical that we prepare ourselves before it is too late and we are lost forever. Jesus is the Light of the world. Turn Him on in your life.

> And there shall be signs in the sun, and in the moon, and in the stars; and upon the earth distress of nations, with perplexity, the sea and the waves roaring; Men's hearts failing them for fear, and for looking after those things which are coming on the earth; for the powers of heaven shall be shaken. And then shall they see the Son of man coming in a cloud with power and great glory. And when these things begin to come to pass, then look up, and lift up your heads; for your redemption draweth nigh.... So likewise ye, when ye see these things come to pass, know ye that the kingdom of God is nigh at hand. Verily I say unto you, this generation shall not pass away,

till all be fulfilled. (Luke 21:25-28, 31, 32)

Wow! What a statement Jesus makes! Do you realize all the implications here? Let us analyze these proclamations of key words that Christ uses. First notice, *begin* and *then* in verse 28. Stated differently, "When these things begin, then look up." Here we see a specific time. In other words, we do not even begin to look up until then. *Then* is what happens in verse 25: signs in the sun, moon, and stars; distress of nations; perplexity; the sea and waves roaring; people's hearts failing for fear because of what is happening on earth; and the powers of heaven shaking. Are these things happening?

Yes, it is true we have seen the fulfillment of prophecy with the signs of the sun, moon, and stars, starting in the early 1800s, and in the great Lisbon earthquake of 1755. These are all signs of the beginning of the end. Do you understand this, the beginning of the end! The Lisbon earthquake happened nearly 250 years ago, and it really shook up that part of the world. How close are we to His coming?

In the book *The Great Controversy*, Ellen White says: "In 1833, two years after Miller began to present in public the evidence of Christ's soon coming, the last of the signs appeared which were promised by the Saviour as tokens of His second advent" (p. 333). Said Jesus, "The stars shall fall from heaven" (Matt. 24:29).

Ellen White says also: "The signs which, He Himself, gave of His coming have been fulfilled, and by the teaching of God's word we may know that the Lord is at the door" (*Christ's Object Lessons*, p. 227). Let's examine this further.

The first of the signs given in Matthew 24:29 is the falling of the stars, which was fulfilled in 1833, as we just read. There was to be a darkening of the sun and the effects in the moon, mentioned in Revelation 6:12, 13—which was fulfilled in 1780 (*The Great Controversy*, p. 308)—and the great Lisbon earthquake, which was in 1755 (*The Great Controversy*,

p. 304). Consequently, we have the beginning of the signs in 1755 and the last of the signs in 1833.

The overview of all this is that the signs that Jesus prophesied were fulfilled in a seventy-eight-year period. This prediction marked the beginning of the end, but it also marked the end of papal persecution upon God's people, which had continued for 1,260 years. This cruelty ended in 1798, when the papal supremacy was broken by Napoleon. This also marked the beginning of a new significance to the world, known as the judgment-hour message. This focal point began in 1844, as recorded in Daniel: "Unto two thousand and three hundred days [literal years]; then shall the sanctuary [heavenly] be cleansed" (Dan. 8:14). This profound prophecy dates the end time. Dear friends, we are living in the time of cleansing, an era when God will purify His church (people), and all the things of the world will not change the fact that God will classify everyone.

Look up and take a stand for God. Do not get trapped with your head hanging. Turn the light on in your life. For nearly 250 years, "God's people" have been looking up because now is the "then" time that Jesus prophesied.

To emphasize it even further, Jesus not only tells us to look up, but to "lift up your heads; for your redemption draweth nigh" (Luke 21:28). Now here is another key word, *nigh*. In Matthew 24:33 and Mark 13:28 Jesus uses the word *near*, which in the Greek language is identified as *eggus*, meaning *near* or *nigh*. If we look at other texts it might help to understand what Jesus meant when He said "nigh." How close can the coming of Christ be without it actually happening? Is the Father about to speak?

Jesus said, "This generation shall not pass, till all these things be done" (Mark 13:30). What is a generation? What kind of a generation was Jesus referring to in this passage? A biblical generation is the age of a man when his first son is born. For instance, if Abraham was 100 years old when Isaac was born, one generation would equal 100 years. According to Genesis 15:13-16, God's people were in bondage 400 years. Furthermore, the Bible states that four generations had passed before God's people were released from oppression. Therefore, the average age of a man would be 100 years old when his first son was born. Today *The Webster's Dictionary* acknowledges the normal age of a man at the birth of his firstborn to be thirty years old.

Consider this. What Christ was referring to was a different type of generation, not a father-son generation. What if He intended for an age to be a generation. In all the references given in Matthew, Mark, and Luke to this prophecy, the word *generation* is taken from the Greek word *genea*, meaning both *literal generation* and *age*. So let us read the text this way, "This **age** shall not pass away until all is done."

The word *generation* is used in the same manner in the book *Christ's Object Lessons*: "In every age there is a new development of truth, a new message of God to the people of that generation" (p. 127). We know that since the year 1844, God has dispensed a conclusive message to anyone who wants to understand the truth. Therefore, we can surmise it is the length of time that exists during the deliverance of that message is what Jesus meant when He said, "generation." Namely, 1844 to the end, when all will be done.

In Genesis 2:4, this statement is recorded concerning the first week of creation, "These are the generations of the heavens and of the earth when they were created." The book *Patriarchs and Prophets* makes reference to this. "Each day was called a generation, because that in it God generated, or produced, some new portion of His work" (p. 112). So here we find that *generation* is merely a frame of time.

The point is, *generation* can mean different measures of time, as well as different genealogical successions, and it appears that in the prophecy, Jesus was telling us about a particular age, which is not bound to the rule of the father-son genealogical time frame.

This appears to be verified by the fact that the "powers of heaven" (Luke 21:26) have not yet been shaken. The darkening of the sun is not the same as "being shaken." The moon turning to blood or the falling of stars is not the same event. However, the Bible says they will be shaken. Has that happened yet?

Ellen White wrote a helpful explanation:

> I saw that when the Lord said "heaven," in giving the signs recorded by Matthew, Mark, and Luke, He meant heaven, and when He said "earth" He meant earth. The powers of heaven are the sun, moon, and stars. They rule the heavens. The powers of earth are those that rule on earth. The powers of heaven will be shaken at the voice of God. Then the sun, moon, and stars will be moved out of their places. They will not pass away, but be shaken by the voice of God. (*Early Writings*, p. 41)

Did you get it? The powers of heaven are shaken by the voice of God! Obviously, this has not happened yet. Please understand the falling of the stars, the sun darkening, and the moon turning to blood are different events from the powers of heaven being shaken.

So where are we in the stream of events? We are in the last half of Luke 21:25 and the first half of Luke 21:26. This is what is happening now, distress of nations, perplexity, sea and waves roaring, and men's hearts literally failing because of what is happening on earth. How long will this continue? It is very, very, very close, but nobody knows the exact time when God will speak, the powers of heaven will shake, and Jesus will come.

At this point in our understanding, we must realize the importance of lifting our heads and looking toward the heavens, watching and praying, preparing and trusting in God because the full intensity of these conditions has not yet materialized.

Yes, friend, many signs have already been fulfilled marking the beginning of the great Advent movement, but the darkest hour, the greatest tribulation is all yet to come before we hear the voice of God emerging toward this world and shaking the universe and everything in it. The seas will roar, and the mountains will be moved. When God's voice is heard, two things will happen: it will confirm the classification of who God's people are, and it will move us directly to the glorious appearing of our Savior and King.

We have not seen anything yet! There will be a fanfare such as never witnessed on this earth. All that can be moved will be moved. Be ye therefore ready at all times. The gleams of the golden morning are fast approaching.

It is time to be classified as a child of God so you can be accounted worthy to escape this world and hear the voice of God reveal His secret about the return of Jesus."

# Chapter Seven

# Thank God for The Lost

The tax collectors and sinners (others) had all gathered together to hear Jesus preach. Jesus was love, and He taught that all of us should love one another. It was hard for some people to understand how Christ could fellowship with publicans and sinners. The Pharisees asked the disciples why their Master ate with publicans and sinners? Jesus overheard the conversation with the Pharisees and answered, "They that be whole need not a physician, but they that are sick. But go ye and learn what that meaneth, I will have mercy, and not sacrifice: for I am not come to call the righteous, but sinners to repentance" (Matt. 9:11-13). What they all failed to realize was that Christ was the Messiah. Love, compassion, and mercy were His character.

As we reflect on Jesus' declaration that He has come to call sinners to repentance, let us look at a few more stories and parables from the Gospels.

In the Gospel of Matthew, Jesus says: "Take heed that ye despise not one of these little ones; for I say unto you, that in heaven their angels do always behold the face of my Father which is in heaven. For the Son of man is come to save that which was lost" (18:10, 11). Does this mean that the sinners have angels in heaven representing them? Those thieves, liars, prostitutes, cheaters, money grabbers, and Sabbath breakers—you mean to tell me that they all have angels in heaven?

**Pause now:** Take a moment to open your Bible and read Matthew 18:10-14 and Luke 15.

In this parable of the sheep; the sheep represent people. So Jesus says, What if you have some sheep and one gets lost, wouldn't you go out and find the lost one? That is the way your Heavenly Father is, He does not want anyone to die and when a sheep, or repentant sinner, is saved, everyone is happy.

Then Jesus goes on about a man with two sons. One goes away with a lot of money, and the other one stays home with a lot of money. Their dad goes out every day to look for the son who left, to welcome him back home. Every day he is there, looking no matter what until he finally sees his son return. The father throws a party to welcome his son back home.

Or suppose that a woman has ten silver coins and loses one. Would she not sweep the house clean to find that coin? Then, when it is found, she rejoices. Jesus says "that there is rejoicing in the presence of the angels of God over one sinner who repents" (Luke 15:10, NKJV).

What do all these parables have in common? They all refer to the lost and to being found.

First, notice that all these lost subjects were once within the ark of safety, so to speak. These lost objects were all part of something. The sheep was part of the fold, the son was part of the family, and the coin was part of the household. These parables are metaphors of being members of God's family. Unfortunately, having left for one reason or another, they are now lost—a change of classification.

Have you ever been lost, friend? Maybe you are lost now, even as you read this sentence. Guess what? Someone is looking for you! Do you realize that the lost ones, by way of being identified and sought after by their Maker, have opened the door for themselves, as well as others, to receive the biggest blessing heaven can bestow on them? Yes! It is called being found—reclassification and salvation! Were it not for at least one who was lost and then found, we would not have known there was a way back to safety.

Now, let us look at this more closely. We have a lost sheep, a lost person, and a lost coin. The sheep knew it was lost and dying, but could not do anything about it. It was helpless in its self-will, entangled in the underbrush, and confused as to which direction was home. It became scared and was unable to do anything about his situation except for one thing, and that was bah, bah, and bah he did. The sheep, in spite of its helpless situation, had an automatic built-in alarm that started sounding bah, bah. When the shepherd heard its call, he came to rescue it. Sometimes in humanity's helpless condition, all one has to do is cry out for help. You can think of it as praying.

In the parable of the lost son, the son was lost and dying but did not realize it until he became hungry and thirsty. He knew where home was and how to get there. He deliberately chose the life he wanted of rebellion and riotous living, and now, after all was gone, he became hungry and started longing for home. He came to his senses and realized that he was destitute and without hope. The Bible says that "he came to himself" (Luke 15:17). Could it be that he was lost within himself? Could it be that because of selfishness, greed, and love for excitement, he had lost his reasoning? Then, when all was gone and he came to his senses, he decided to do something about his condition. He knew where hope was; he then went back home. He remembered that his father loved him. He recollected the memory of security. He evaluated the hopelessness of his present situation against the hope of his father's acceptance and knew that home was where he should really go. He made the right decision and went home to Father. Have you left your heavenly Father? Please, return home. He is waiting for you.

Now, the lost coin did not know it was lost. Even if it did, it could not do anything about it. It could not think for itself, make noise, or even move. It just lay there totally helpless, waiting to be found. The owner of the coin searched endlessly and tirelessly because it had a value to the owner. Are you a lost coin waiting to be found by your owner, Jesus? He is searching for you right now because He considers you valuable to Him.

Let us think of these three parables as representing three classes of lost people.

1. The sheep that knows it is lost but is helpless.
2. The son who knows he is lost and can do something about it.
3. The coin that does not know it is lost and can do nothing about it.

Now, let this message sink in: all were found, regardless of their situation.

Does the list, Sin, Savior, and Salvation, communicate to you anything other than the fact that all these words begin with the letter *s*? Let us briefly define each one.

1. Sin: separates us from the Savior and causes us to be lost.
2. Savior: provides a way to be found.
3. Salvation: continual joy and security of being found.

Now tell me, why are so many people lost? The Bible says, "For many are called, but few are chosen" (Matt. 22:14). Let us compare this to Matt. 7:13, 14: "Enter ye in at the strait gate; for wide is the gate, and broad is the way that leadeth to destruction, and many there be which go in threat: Because strait is the gate, and narrow is the way, which leadeth unto life, and few there be that find it." Many people are lost because of continual resistance on their part. The emphasis here is not on resistance, but on continual. The sheep showed no resistance and was saved. The coin gave no resistance and was saved. The son showed much resistance but finally stopped resisting, and was saved. Even though we may show resistance at times, it does not have to mean we are lost! We can come to a point of non-resistance and be saved.

This is precisely what God's Word tells us: "Let every soul be subject unto the higher powers. For there is no power but of God: the powers that be are ordained of God. Whosoever therefore resisteth the power, resisteth the ordinance of God: and they that resist shall receive to themselves damnation" (Rom. 13:1, 2). It is by our continual, never-ending resistance that we actually condemn ourselves.

Think about the days of Noah. "And God saw that the wickedness of man was great in the earth, and that every imagination of the thoughts of his heart was only evil continually" (Gen. 6:5). Because their resistance and thus their wickedness was continual, they became destroyed.

Damnation = Condemnation = Without Christ = Lost.

Where are you, my friend? Are you continually resisting? Please, discontinue your resistance and get re-classified.

However, continual can be a good characteristic, if you want to continually magnify God. "Let all those that seek thee rejoice and be glad in thee: let such as love thy salvation say continually, The Lord be magnified" (Ps. 40:16). God will then continually preserve you in your salvation. "Withhold not thou thy tender mercies from me, O Lord: let thy loving kindness and thy truth continually preserve me" (Ps. 40:11).

Realize something else here: in order for something or someone to be saved, someone else had to put forth energy. The shepherd went out to look for the sheep, and he found it. The father went out to look for his son, and he found him. The lady looked for her coin, and she found it. Perhaps, someone is looking for you, too. Please, do not resist.

Now that we have drawn some lessons about the lost, as told in the parables, let us think more about the finder of the lost. First, there is the shepherd. "Now the God of peace, that brought again from the dead our Lord Jesus, that great shepherd of the sheep, through the blood of the everlasting covenant" (Heb. 13:20). The Bible depicts Jesus as the shepherd. "I am the good shepherd, and know My sheep" (John 10:14).

Next, there is a father. "But to us there is but one God, the Father, of whom are all things, and we in Him; and one Lord Jesus Christ, by whom are all things, and we by Him" (1 Cor. 8:6). This depicts God the Father, as the Father, which should be no surprise to us.

However, have you ever noticed that the Bible imbues the Holy Spirit with female, especially maternal, attributes? It is as if the Holy Spirit plays the role of a woman. Let me explain this one. Children are not born of men; they are born of women. The Bible uses the birth experience as a symbol of being born again spiritually in Him. One cannot be born physically without a mother nor be born again spiritually without the Holy Spirit. "…Except a man be born again he cannot see the kingdom of God…. Except a man be born of water and of the Spirit, he cannot enter into the kingdom of God" (John 3:3-5). Interestingly, Jesus refers to the Holy Spirit as Comforter (John 14:26).

No, it does not say that the Holy Spirit is a woman, but rather implies that the Holy Spirit often plays the role of a woman, the role of a mother the same way that Jesus takes on the role of Shepherd and Son. Remember that both man and woman, together, were created in the image of God (Gen. 1:27). Therefore, the Godhead must possess both male and female characteristics; recognizing one without the other would paint an incomplete picture of God.

In the parables we find the Holy Trinity going out of their way and putting forth much effort to seek and save the lost no matter what the circumstance. And so we see Jesus as the Shepherd and the Son, The Father as the Father, and the Holy Spirit as the mother. This Holy Trinity is working together for the salvation of mankind.

When Jesus was here on earth, He advocated the Holy Trinity. The Holy Trinity came to earth with Jesus to seek and to save the lost. "For the Son of Man is come to save that which was lost" (Matt. 18:11, NKJV).

If you or someone you know is resisting God, do not give up hope.

No matter what the classification, all can be re-classified (saved). This is what God's love is entirely about; God's love can completely change your life. However, there is one thing God will not do; God will not force you to stop resisting. This is a decision only you can make.

Yes, thank God for the lost. Thank Him for the parable of the *lost* sheep, for the parable of the *lost* son, and the parable of the *lost* coin. All the parables cry aloud, there is hope; if one is lost, one can be found!

**How are you classified?**

Maybe you are one of the ninety-nine sheep safe in the fold, or maybe you are the brother's son at home showing jealousy and bitterness, or maybe you are one of those who became separated, or fell be the wayside. Whatever your classification, remember one thing: Jesus wants you to be saved. Please do not continually resist!

*Now* is the day of salvation. Yesterday is gone, and tomorrow may not come, but now is always here. Jesus is always here, waiting for you to stop resisting and start insisting on re-classifying yourself. Why would you not redirect yourself to God right now? What do you have to lose? Heaven is cheap enough no matter what you have to sacrifice for it now.

# Chapter Eight

# The Mountain

Picture the scene: Jesus is in the garden praying. Where are His friends? Sleeping, of course! Three times (remember this number), He goes to them for help and support and finds them asleep. Who is praying for Jesus? No one! Whom is Jesus praying for? Everyone!

**Pause now:** Read John 17 and meditate on it.

John 17 is the real Lord's Prayer! This is the prayer that Jesus prays just before He goes to the cross, and while He is in the garden, Jesus prays for Himself and begins to climb the mountain, His Mountain. So earnest and sincere, so taxing and draining, so caring and concerned, so intimate and personal is the struggle He feels. It literally causes Him to sweat blood and disfigures His face to the point that the disciples barely recognize Him. So seemingly unbearable is this experience that *three* times Jesus asks for this cup to pass from Him.

Enter Judas and the mob. Do you suppose Judas readily recognizes Jesus with the anguished look on His face and the blood streaming down? Furthermore, it is dark in the night, and Judas must look closely to make sure it is Jesus he kisses. Have you ever kissed anyone with blood on his or her face? How repulsive! Judas must have really had to put forth much effort to betray Jesus. Do you suppose he got blood on his lips? What do you think was going through the mind of Judas when Jesus picked up the bloody ear that Peter had cut off the soldier and put it back on his head, completely healing him? What a scene. Read it in

Mark 14:32-47 and Matthew 26:36-56. Oh, what a wonderful God and Savior, amid all His sufferings. He still thinks of the good of others and helps them. Oh, to be more like Jesus.

And, now Jesus is taken from court to court to court, to face (1) Caiaphas, the high priest, (2) Pilate the governor, and (3) Herod the king. There is that number three again. Look at Luke 22:66, 23:1, 6, 7 and John 18:24, 28.

While Jesus appears before Caiaphas, something else is happening. Peter is watching from afar. You can read the story in Matthew 26:62-75 and Mark 14:60-72. A lady approaches Peter and says, "I saw you with Jesus," and Peter replies, "I do not know what you are saying." And now Peter begins to climb his mountain.

Peter denies Jesus *three* times, and then he hears a rooster crow, and then a deafening sound of Jesus' words rings through his head: "you will deny Me three times." So Peter "went out and wept bitterly" (Matt. 26:75, NKJV). Can you imagine the weight in Peter's heart?

It is interesting that the word *bitter* is used here. Bitter is usually associated with an unpleasant taste in the mouth, and it was from Peter's mouth that the words of denial came *three* times, which caused him a most unpleasant experience. You see, Peter had classified himself as apart from Jesus, not as a part of Jesus. Circumstances changed his behavior. His actions caused a mountain in his life.

Circumstances can cause us to do strange things. *Strange*, meaning *unusual* or *out of character*, even to the ones we love most. Peter's experience demonstrates this. Fortunately, in these moments of weeping and remorse (sorrowful repentance) on his mountain, Peter truly found Jesus. Even though Peter's mountain experience left him with scars, Peter's undying love for Jesus gave him victory.

Are you on a mountain of unpleasant, bitter experiences? You can find Jesus there just as Peter did, by rekindling the love for Him in your heart.

Night has passed into the late morning hours, and by now Jesus is weak, faint, and weary from lack of sleep and a heavy loss of blood from His beating. His whole body is bruised, torn, punctured, and beaten from a reed. He was spat upon, cursed at, totally humiliated, and mocked. How much endurance can a man have?

Then they lay the cross on Him, and He faints and falls beneath the heavy beam. Again they put it on His back, and again He faints. The *third* time it is picked up, but this time it is not given to Jesus because He is unable to bear the burden. One called Simon from Cyrene is now chosen to carry the cross.

Simon was not yet a follower of Christ. However, in bearing the cross, Simon willingly and compassionately followed Jesus to Calvary, and together they climbed the mountain. This experience proved to be a blessing to Simon. It led him to take upon himself the cross of Christ by choice and to cheerfully stand beneath its burden. Simon found a new classification in his encounter with Jesus and became a follower of Christ.

This is a reminder of Matthew 16:24, where Jesus said, "If any man will come after me, let him deny himself and take up his cross and follow me." Jesus wants us to re-classify ourselves with Him. He will climb the mountain with us and guarantee life. Did you get that? He guarantees life! Mark 8:36 says, "For will it profit a man if he gains the whole world, and loses his own soul." Believe it, friend, Jesus wants to give you life and rewards, but it takes acceptance and nonresistance on our part and a willingness to be re-classified as a follower of Jesus.

Speaking of the cross, we find another word that can be used for *cross,* and that is *stake.* One of the meanings of the word *stake* is, "that which is pledged." In the early years of the American west there was a gold rush to California. Those who looked for gold were often times called prospectors. Some of those prospectors were poor and needed someone to lend them money for food and supplies while they looked for gold. Then, if and when they found the gold, the money was returned to the lender. This was known as a stake. Trust was a very important ingredient in this kind of relationship, and a pledge had to be made by the prospector to repay the one who provided the means. A pledge also had to be made by the provider to supply the means to the prospector. It goes both ways.

Think of Jesus as the provider, the one supplying our needs. He made a pledge and hung on a stake to guarantee us the provisions of eternal life with Him in His heavenly mansion. Yes, true eternal life is a free gift from God—we cannot buy it or pay Him back for it—but He does ask for a pledge. He tells us to take up our cross and follow Him. Jesus is saying to us, "Take a stake in Me, trust Me, follow Me, and I will guarantee you a city with gold abundantly." Jesus wants our pledge to love Him and to be faithful to Him. He was willing to take a stake in us. It goes both ways.

"Thou shalt love the Lord thy God with all thine heart, and with all thy soul, and with all thy might" (Deut. 6:5).

"Be thou faithful unto death, and I will give thee a crown of life" (Rev. 2:10).

If you are on a mountain of crisis, please remember three things:

1. Your mountain is only temporary, but eternity with God is permanent.
2. Jesus wants you to trust in Him and follow Him daily.
3. Jesus will guarantee you eternal life with Him.

Remember: (1) mountains, (2) trust, and (3) guarantee. We must have mountains as Christ demonstrated so we can develop trust in Him as He did in the Father. Then He will guarantee us salvation as we follow Him into paradise.

As we return to the scenes of Calvary, try to picture the suffering He endured as the soldiers nailed Him down to the cross. Can you see the two thieves fighting with resistance? Can you hear them cursing and yelling at the soldiers?

Now, look at Jesus yielding himself up willingly, and as they spike Him down, the only sound that is heard from His lips are the deep agonizing groans of horrible pain. And then there is that look on His face that catches the attention of everyone, and it says, "This blood is for you."

As they lift the cross and thrust it into the hole, it tears His flesh and pulls on the bones. After all this torture, the words that come from Jesus' lips are captivating, "Father forgive them" (Luke 23:34), as if to say, "Forgive all of them who have ever sinned against us." That means you, the person who reads these words, everyone, including me; this blood is for all of us.

Then someone mockingly shouts, "If you are the Son of God, come down from the cross" and save yourself (Matt 27:40, NKJV). The people did not understand that it was precisely because He *was* the Son of God that He could not come down from the cross. A multitude of angels were there, and they wanted to rescue Jesus, but He could not be rescued; it was the divine plan. Jesus had to stay and do it all for us because God is love. He is the source of love, He is the greatest love, and there is no greater love than when a man lays down his life for a friend. It was His love for us that restrained Him from leaving the cross. It was His love for us that made Him willing to die on that mountain. Jesus is waiting for you to respond to that love. Come to His mountain and meet Him there.

Something else happened that day on Calvary. From the mountain of death came forth life. A new life for all of us was born from Christ's death.

Now, picture Jesus. He is hanging there with His head on His chest, and He is barely breathing; His eyes are closed. He is ready to die, and He hears these precious words. He longs to hear each one of us say these words, the words worth dying for. Listen to what Jesus hears.

"But the other answering rebuked him, saying, Dost thou not fear God, seeing thou art in the same condemnation? And we indeed justly; for we receive the due reward of our deeds: but this man hath done nothing amiss. And he said unto Jesus, Lord, remember me when thou comest into thy kingdom" (Luke 23:40-43).

Instantly, Jesus' eyes open wide, His head is lifted up, His adrenaline starts flowing, He turns His head toward the thief, and His reaction is vocalized: "Yes! Yes! Believe me when I tell you today, because it is true, you will be with me in paradise."

Incidentally, this word *paradise* means *park* or *garden ground*. Revelation 2:3 tells us that the tree of life is in the midst of the garden of God. Jesus guaranteed that this man will be in the garden of God where there is eternal life.

Everything Jesus had gone through up to this point was taking its toll on Him. Our sins were a well of darkness between Him and the Father to the extent that Jesus felt the separation. For the first time in the history of eternity, something had come between Him and the Father. Oh, what loneliness, what heartache, what grief. For the first time, Jesus feels forsaken, and He cries out, "Father why, why, why have you forsaken me."

And so, through the lips of the thief, God manifests the presence of His Spirit, for it is by the Holy Spirit that all are drawn to Him. Now Jesus feels the presence of the Father in the testimony of the re-classified man hanging next to Him. On that day at that moment, that man found salvation in Jesus. And Jesus found the Father and the Holy Spirit in that man on the mountain. Could it be that this was the experience that reassured Jesus that His Father was still with Him on the mountain? Jesus wants to reassure you of His love for you and of his promise in your life.

Have you found Jesus on your mountain? Do you understand what the cross is all about? Are you willing to take a stake in Jesus?

He was spreading His arms out telling us how much He loved us, and we nailed His hands down to the cross. Take a stake in Jesus today. He took a stake for you.

Listen, my friend, sin separates us from God just as it separated Jesus as He hung on the cross. But they were not His sins; they were ours.

If you are living a life of sin that is separating you from God, give it up to Jesus and trade it in for His 1-2-3 program of eternal life;

1. Justification: seeking forgiveness and re-classifying yourself with Him.
2. Sanctification: Be determined to live your life His way not your way and set yourself aside from worldly use to His use.
3. Glorification: Let Him change you to be like Him and live with Him eternally.

# Chapter Nine

# Sleeping Sickness and Ho-Hummers

Let us explore and ponder Jesus' description of the spiritual condition of the world and the church prior to His return. Jesus offers several illustrations that paint a clear picture, cautioning us to not be self-deceived as to our own condition and urging us to accept the necessary provisions that He so graciously and pleadingly offers.

In His discourse about all that would take place from His ascension to the end of time, Christ makes a very instructive parallel between His second coming and the story of Noah.

> But as the days of Noah were, so also will the coming of the Son of Man be. For as in the days before the flood, they were eating and drinking, marrying and giving in marriage, until the day that Noah entered the ark, and did not know until the flood came and took them all away, so also will the coming of the Son of Man be. (Matt. 24:37-39, NKJV).

In this text "the days of Noah" do not refer to Noah's childhood or his young adult life or when he was even 300 or 400 years old. "The days of Noah" refer to a very specific period of time. The verse says the days of Noah that were "before the flood."

Now, this word *before* can mean many things; however, in this context, it comes from the Greek word *pro*, which is to say, *in front of*. When something or someone is referred to as being *in front of* you, it does not mean a million miles away; it means right there, near you. And so we can understand this text to mean that the "days of Noah" are those directly in front of the flood, during that time period. It is important to understand what the root of the word *before* means, because Jesus recalls a specific time in Noah's life and the destruction of earth then and compares it to a precise time in our lives and the destruction of the earth with the second coming of Jesus.

Basically, Jesus is saying that life will go on as usual. It is believed that Noah preached approximately 120 years that the flood was coming, yet people went on as usual, living in sin and not repenting. "And it repented [shamed] the LORD that he had made man on the earth, and it grieved [caused him deep sorrow and distress] him at his heart" (Gen. 6:6). Can you think of another time when God experienced the shame of the world, a time that caused Him deep sorrow and distress? What about the cross? God depicts the lifestyle of people at the time of the flood and applies it to the lifestyle at the time of Jesus' second coming. Are we any different than the people of Noah's time?

Let's delve into another of Jesus' teachings pertaining to the end time. It was twilight. Jesus and His disciples were sitting in the grass. From across the hillside, they could see a house that was lit up, and in the house were some people milling around in the dwelling. Something seemed to be going on that was very exciting. As the light streamed through the cracks of the doorways and the windows, it appeared that a small company of women were waiting for something or someone.

Christ and His disciples sat there on the hillside looking at this scene, and Jesus thought that this would be a good time to teach His disciples another valuable lesson. The scene they were watching was part of the preparations for a wedding, which was soon to take place.

In many parts of the east, when people prepare for a wedding, they do so in the evening. The bridegroom goes to meet the bride, and it is extremely important to have light bearers to light the path so that everyone can see where they are going. The torches that are carried are larger than ordinary indoor lamps and they require a more plenteous amount of oil to burn them because they glow brighter with more fire. Along with the torch, it is necessary that another vessel of oil be carried with it in the event it is needed.

Jesus says:

> Then [just before His second coming] shall the king-dom of heaven [kingdom within you] be likened unto ten virgins [the true blue, unadulterated with false doctrine people], which took [possessed] their lamps [lights], and went forth to meet the bridegroom [Jesus]. And five of them were wise [mindful], and five were foolish [dull, stupid]. They that were foolish took their lamps, and took no oil with them. But the wise took oil in their vessels with their lamps. While the bride-groom [Jesus] tarried [delayed], they all slumbered and slept [became indifferent]. And at midnight [the darkest hour] there was a cry made [announcement], Behold, the bridegroom cometh; go ye out to meet him. Then all the virgins arose, and trimmed [set in or-der] their lamps. And the foolish said to the wise, Give us your oil; for our lamps are gone out. But the wise answered, saying, Not so; lest there be not enough for us and you: but go ye rather to them that sell, and buy

for yourselves. And, while they went to buy, the bridegroom came; and they that were ready went in with him to the marriage: and the door was shut. Afterward came also the other virgins saying, Lord, Lord, open to us. But He answered and said, Verily I say unto you, I know you not. Watch therefore, for ye know neither the day, nor the hour wherein the Son of man cometh. (Matt. 25:1-13)

Jesus wanted to illustrate to His disciples, through the parable of the ten virgins, the importance of being filled with the Holy Spirit (oil), thus having the kingdom of heaven within us. Therefore, this represents the importance of readiness while waiting for Jesus to come just as the virgins were waiting for the bridegroom.

As we look at this parable, we can compare it to Matthew 24, Jesus' discourse on His second coming. The condition of humankind that Jesus paints in Matthew 24 is identified in the parable of the ten virgins also; it's a sleeping condition (Matt. 25:5). It says they "slumbered." Slumber implies negligence, which means the virgins were careless and they slept. They were indifferent. Does this remind you of Laodicea mentioned in Revelation 3:14-22? The sleeping problem in the parable communicates that the virgins were negligent or indifferent to the coming of their bridegroom.

Really, the indifference portrayed in the parable of the ten virgins is the same indifference at the time of the flood and will be the same indifference at the time of His second coming. They will be sick, wretched, miserable, poor, blind, and naked with the "sleeping sickness." The virgins were sick in their minds, thinking they could get by with a minimum of provisions. They became wretched because they ran out of the necessary provisions. They were miserable because they could not secure more provisions. They were poor in spirit and of supply. They were left naked of everything.

Did you catch the "Then" in the opening line to the parable of the ten virgins, "Then shall the kingdom of heaven" (Matt. 25:1)? This is the time just before Jesus comes, and this is relative to the "then" time we read about in Matthew 24:21, 22, which says: "For then shall be great tribulation, such as was not since the beginning of the world to this time, no, nor ever shall be. And except those days should be shortened, there should no flesh be saved: but for the elect's sake those days shall be shortened." The question is, how do we know both of the "then" times are referring to the same era?

We know there was a great tribulation during the destruction of Jerusalem, when the Jews and Christians were tortured and crucified; but that was not the "then" time, because we know another, even greater, tribulation occurred during the rule of the Papal Roman Empire, which we call the Dark Ages. But even that time was not the "then" time Matthew 24:21 refers to, because we are still here several hundred years after the Dark Ages. The three angels' messages have not yet been proclaimed, nor has the outpouring of the latter rain occurred in its fullness in those times of history.

Verse 21 says there will never be destruction as great as that one. During this time of destruction, there will be a group of people called "the elect." How is it determined who the elect are? There is only one way to become part of the elect, and that is by the sealing of the Holy Spirit, just before the close of probation, when all become permanently classified.

> At that time shall Michael stand up, the great prince which standeth for the children of thy people [remnant]: and there shall be a time of trouble, such as never was since there was a nation [great tribulation] even to that same time: and at that time thy people [elect]

shall be delivered, everyone that shall be found written in the book. (Dan. 12:1)

Now, listen, friend; this has not happened, so we have to conclude that Matthew 24:21-27 is yet to come.

Listen to the words of Ellen White:

> When the third angel's message closes, mercy no longer pleads for the guilty inhabitants of the earth. The people of God have accomplished their work.... As the angels of God cease to hold in check the fierce winds of human passion, all the elements of strife will be let loose. The whole world will be involved in ruin more terrible than that which came upon Jerusalem of old.... There are forces now ready, and only waiting the divine permission, to spread desolation everywhere. (*The Great Controversy*, pp. 613, 614).

If this does not sound as if the greatest tribulation that ever hit this earth is still to come, then we are just fooling ourselves.

Do you understand why Jesus compares the two "then's" to the greatest time period? It is when the greatest tribulation of all comes that the greatest of all tests comes to determine the greatest of all faith and loyalty to develop the purest virgin for the Bridegroom.

During this time, who are the survivors? Who are the victorious? There are two classifications here, the living righteous (144,000), and the dead righteous (the martyrs), but all represent the five wise virgins, and all are overcomers; all are victorious, and all are survivors from the evil one, even though many die a temporary death at that time.

The difference between the 144,000 and the martyrs is that the 144,000 have a greater testing and a more purifying experience, enabling them to live in the sight of God without an intercessor during the seven last plagues (God's wrath), after the close of probation.

Understand here that the "great tribulation" and the "wrath of God" are two separate events. The great tribulation is before the close of probation, and the wrath of God is after probation closes. The great tribulation purifies the true church, and the wrath of God destroys the false church. However, it is all classified as the time of trouble.

Remember, Jesus said that His church would be like the parable of the ten virgins; five were foolish and five were wise. In order to help us understand our classification and whether or not we need to be re-classified, let's take a look at what the parables illustrate and represent. Remember, now, this parable represents the condition of God's church prior to being purified just before Jesus returns to earth.

There are many representations in the parable. The following is a list of the first five.

1. The ten virgins represent purity, and in this parable, virginity is a symbol of a pure faith. In Scripture, God's church represents a virgin woman; see Revelation 12. The apostle Paul wrote: "For I am jealous over you with godly jealousy: for I have espoused you to one husband, so that I might present you as a chaste virgin to Christ" (2 Cor. 11:2). Jesus uses the virgins to describe His church at the "then" time to be revealing the pure faith. Therefore, the ten virgins equal the pure faith church. However, only five virgins end up possessing the pure faith.

2. The lamps symbolize the Holy Bible and the Spirit of Prophecy. In Psalm 119:105 we read, "Thy word is a lamp unto my feet and a light unto my path." Without question, we all believe this refers to the Holy Bible. But the Bible also says, "Here is the patience of the saints; here are they [the virgins] that keep the commandments of God and the faith of Jesus" (Rev. 14:12).

What is the faith of Jesus? Is it not His testimony? We read in Revelation 19:10, "For the testimony of Jesus is the spirit of prophecy." The remnant "keep the commandments, and have the testimony of Jesus Christ" (Rev. 12:17).

Therefore, we can conclude that the Word we call the Bible, and the Spirit of Prophecy that Ellen White represents, are the earmarks of the pure faith church symbolized by the lamp. "The Lord has given a lesser light [Ellen White] to lead men and women to the greater light [Holy Bible] (*Evangelism*, p. 257). The Old Testament, New Testament, and the testimonies of Ellen White are lights, all represented by the lamp.

Let us make no mistake, friends. The light given to us through Ellen White is as much a part of the Word of God as the light given through the people who wrote the Scriptures and proclaimed the true message of God in their time.

Elijah proclaimed it! At a time when Israel was all wrapped up in idolatry and the ways of the world, God sent Elijah with a message for them. "Ye have forsaken the Commandments of the Lord, and thou hast followed Baalim.... And Elijah came unto all the people, and said, how long halt ye between two opinions? if the Lord be God, follow Him: but if Baal, then follow him.... I, even I only, remain a prophet of the Lord" (1 Kings 18:18-22).

Elijah was a messenger of the Lord, sent to the people of Israel with a message of repentance and restoration. Israel had breached their covenant with God and refused to follow the Ten Commandments. They worshiped Baal instead of God and followed the ways of the world. It was Elijah's mission to guide God's people back to the ways of their Creator.

Isaiah was another whom God used to serve Him. "The voice of one crying in the wilderness: "Prepare the way of the Lord; Make straight in the desert a highway for our God (Isa. 40:3, NKJV). "Thou shalt be called, The repairer of the breach, The restorer of paths to dwell in" (Isa. 58:12). Again, the "breach" and the "paths" are in reference to the commandments and the worship of God. The next two verses give caution regarding the breaking of the covenant:

> If thou turn away thy foot from the sabbath, from doing thy pleasure on my holy day; and call the sabbath a delight, the holy of the LORD, honourable; and shalt honour him, not doing thine own ways, nor finding thine own pleasure, nor speaking thine own words: Then shalt thou delight thyself in the LORD ... for the mouth of the Lord hath spoken it. (Isa. 58:13, 14)

Isaiah was the mouthpiece, or messenger, of God to bring God's people back to God and His ways. John the Baptist was famous for this very same work.

> In those days came John the Baptist, preaching in the wilderness of Judaea, and saying, Repent ye; for the kingdom of heaven is at hand. For this is he that was spoken of by the prophet Esaias, saying, The voice of one crying in the wilderness, Prepare ye the way of the Lord, make His paths straight. (Matt. 3:1-3).

Isaiah presented God's message to Israel. At the time of this reprimand, Israel had their own set of rules, which was just as much a false system of worship as the worship of Baal. Isaiah prophesied the return of the message in the person of John the Baptist, thus setting the stage for the appearance of

Christ. John was referred to as Elijah because of the message he bore. "Behold, I send my messenger before thy face, which shall prepare thy way before thee.... And if ye will receive it [the message], this is Elias [Elijah] which was for to come" (Matt. 11:10, 14).

Yes, God sent the prophets Moses, Jeremiah, Isaiah, Elisha, Elijah, and John with a special work of reconciliation. God does not leave His people without a messenger, and it is no different in the time when Jesus will return at His second coming. He will lead His people to prepare the way for the second coming with a messenger as well.

> Remember ye the law of Moses my servant, which I commanded unto him in Horeb for all Israel, with the statutes and judgments. Behold, I will send you Elijah the prophet [the messenger] before the coming of the great and dreadful day of the Lord. And, he shall turn the heart of the fathers to the children, and the heart of the children to their fathers, lest I come and smite the earth with a curse. (Mal. 4:4-6)

Here we are, friend, right "before" the coming of the Lord—the time when God's people once again resemble the world more than they do Him, when they have their own set of "laws" that govern their religious ways, rather than yield to His ways. This is the time when God's people need a messenger of the Lord. This is the time when God fulfills the prophecy of Malachi 4:5. Do you recognize it? Make no mistake about it; God has sent His messenger and the completion of this prophecy in Ellen White and people like her who are filled with the Holy Spirit. It is time that we recognize that Ellen

White was, without a shadow of a doubt, a prophetess. She was blessed with the gift of prophecy. God is proclaiming to His people: "Repair the breach. Repent, for the Kingdom is at hand. Prepare yourself for the Bridegroom."

Yes, her messages from the Lord are as much a part of the virgins' lamps as what you can read in the Bible. Accept it, believe it, live it, because it is a definite identifying mark of God's last people. "Believe His prophets, so shall ye prosper" (2 Chron. 20:20) "By the lamps is represented the word of God" (*Christ's Object Lessons*, p. 406). Without it you cannot be classified as a remnant.

3.  The light stands for the Word of God. It means being filled with the Holy Spirit and having knowledge of Scripture and a love for the truth. God's followers carry a light to the darkened world. That light is the Word of God in its fullness and entirety. Those who understand and accept the Elijah message will be true light bearers of the third angel's message to the gloomy world. This makes them the light of the world. "Ye are the light of the world" (Matt. 5:14). "Then Jesus said unto them, I am the light of the world; he that followeth me shall not walk in darkness, but shall *have the light* of life" (John 8:12, italics mine).

4.  The oil represents the anointing of the Holy Spirit. "Thou shalt take the anointing oil, and pour it upon his head, and anoint him" (Exod. 29:7). Anointing is a method used to sanctify something or someone. "And thou shalt anoint it, to sanctify it" (Exod. 29:36). To sanctify is to set apart. When something or someone is set apart for God's use, that object or person is for holy use because God is Holy. Therefore, what God sanctifies He sets aside for holy use.

It is by the Holy Spirit that God teaches and uses us. Read, for instance, the following verses: "But the comforter, which is the Holy Ghost, whom the Father will send in My name, He shall teach you all things, and bring all things to your remembrance, whatsoever I have said unto you" (John 14:26). "And they were all filled with the Holy Ghost, and began to speak with other tongues, as the Spirit gave them utterance" (Acts 2:4). "How God anointed Jesus of Nazareth with the Holy Ghost and with power: who went about doing good, and healing all that were oppressed of the devil; for God was with Him" (Acts 10:38).

Do you get the picture yet? To be anointed and set apart with oil is to be filled with the Holy Spirit for God's Holy use. The oil represents the Holy Spirit in the lives of God's people. "The oil is a symbol of the Holy Spirit" (*Christ's Object Lessons*, p. 406).

5.  The vessel symbolizes all ten virgins who had lamps with oil in them. All ten of them had extra vessels, but only five of them had an extra measure of oil that enabled them to go into the marriage.

    Pay attention, now; the lamps were also vessels, which contained oil and the wick. All had the lamp vessel, and all had the extra vessel. Could it be that both vessels represent the people of God just before Jesus comes? The lamp vessels are all who receive the Holy Spirit in their lives when they first come to Christ. It is as though they are lit up with their newfound love, and the Holy Spirit sanctifies them for the Master's use. "If a man therefore purge himself from these, he shall be a vessel unto honour, sanctified, and meet for the master's use, and prepared unto every good work" (2 Timothy 2:21). This is referred to as the early rain experience, or the first outpouring of the Holy Spirit in the life.

    Unfortunately, after a period of time, laziness sets in, and they *all* fall asleep. They all become inactive to the study of the Word and communication through prayer. They become insensitive to the importance of the light they bear—ho-hummers with sleeping sickness.

But what about the other, "extra" vessel? "Each carries a lighted lamp and a small flagon for oil; … But five had neglected to fill their flasks with oil" (*Christ's Object Lessons*, p. 405).

The foolish virgins took no oil with them. They did not fill the extra vessel, which means the vessel was not filled with the "extra" oil. No oil, no Holy Spirit. Their lights went out because they were not prepared for the unexpected delay. But those who thought beforehand had enough oil to keep their lamps burning. The more oil you have, the more you will have of the Holy Spirit because the oil represents the Holy Spirit. This will happen as the latter rain. The extra measure of the Holy Spirit determines who will go into the marriage supper.

What else can we learn from this parable? We can discover that the virgins were not just the bridesmaids; they were *a part of* the bride as well. The Bible tells us—and we have already learned—that Christ's church is His bride, and if the virgins represent the true church then the virgins are also *a part of* the church.

We can also determine that the virgins and the bride were not the only ones in the bridal procession. "The five with lighted lamps joined the throng and entered the house with the bridal train" (*Christ's Object Lessons*, p. 406). Before we can consider who the "throng" is, we need to back up and look at the "cry." "And at midnight there was a cry made, Behold, the bridegroom cometh; go ye out to meet him (Matt. 25:6). It is the cry that woke the virgins up, enabling them to react to the situation at hand. Is it not the Holy Spirit who awakens our spirituality so that we can react to the circumstance? Is it possible that the cry in the night is the Holy Spirit calling all of us to service and duty through the medium of persecution and tribulation, which is represented by the midnight hour?

When the virgins woke up, they all arose and trimmed their lamps, representing a last-minute effort in preparation for the Bridegroom. For a very short period of time, we see the virgins vigorously working to provide a glow for the night. Finally, they discern the importance of the hour. Unfortunately, those who have no oil cannot provide light. Therefore, they can do nothing but leave the scene. "They went to buy" (Matt. 25:10). You would think that they would have realized it was midnight. Consequently, there would be no place to buy oil at that hour. However, in desperation, they went to buy. It is amazing how foolish and confused people become when they are desperate. The five foolish virgins were frantic and went to look for oil. They constitute half of the maidens.

Could it be that about half of the members of the true remnant will be found slumbering without oil? Consequently, they will lose their place at the wedding feast. Dear reader, please study Scripture, pray, and exercise your faith in God so you will not be considered classified among those looking for oil.

In *Christ's Object Lessons*, page 406, Ellen White writes:

> While they went to buy, the procession moved on, and left them behind. The five with lighted lamps joined the throng and entered the house with the bridal train, and the door was shut. When the foolish virgins reached the banqueting hall, they received an unexpected denial. The master of the feast declared, "I know you not." They were left standing without, in the empty street, in the blackness of the night.

The throng previously mentioned represents those who accept the three angels' messages prior to the second coming of Christ to go into the marriage with the five virgins. While all this was happening, here came the foolish virgins to the door, only to be pronounced strangers and denied access. When Jesus comes, the foolish virgins are going to hear those dreadful words from Him: "And then will I profess unto them, I never knew you: depart from me ye that work iniquity" (Matt. 7:23). The empty street and blackness of night is symbolic of their destruction. "Depart from me, ye cursed, into everlasting fire" (Matt. 25:41).

Do you recall when the five foolish asked the wise for oil? "And the wise answered no" (Matt. 25:8, 9). Oh, dear reader, brother and sister, friend and relative of mine, if you do not have your own personal experience (oil) with Jesus, you will not have developed the character that He wants to find when He comes. You cannot have anyone else's experience or character. You must find and develop your own experience and character with your own oil of the Holy Spirit. The Holy Spirit experience is not transferable.

"In the great and measureless gift of the Holy Spirit are contained all of heaven's resources. It is not because of any restriction on the part of God that the riches of His grace do not flow earthward to men. If all were willing to receive, all would become filled with His Spirit" (*Christ's Object Lessons*, p. 419).

Dear reader, I appeal to you. Please acquire, if you haven't already, the book *Christ's Object Lesson*, by Ellen G. White, and read the last chapter, "To Meet the Bridegroom."

Be determined to classify yourself as among the wise.

# Chapter Ten

# Pollution—Solution

The Christian life is definitely not easy. Staying true and pressing on after our initial decision to follow Christ does not come without its struggles. A great many influences, interests, ideals, beliefs, goals, activities, duties, demands, and even persons can obstruct—or pollute—our decision and desire to love and live for Christ. Fortunately, Christ not only provides us with the ability to discern such efforts of Satan to deceive and derail us but also offers us ways—solutions—to overcome them.

Let's read an important passage in the Spirit of Prophecy that diagnoses many a Christian's pollutions in life:

> Many of the people of God are stupefied by the spirit of the world, and are denying their faith by their works. They cultivate a love for money, for houses and lands, until it absorbs the powers of mind and being, and shuts out love for the Creator and for souls for whom Christ died. The God of this world has blinded their eyes; their eternal interests are made secondary; and brain, bone, and muscle are taxed to the utmost to increase their worldly possessions. And all this accumulation of cares and burdens is borne in direct violation of the injunction of Christ, who said, "Lay not up for

yourselves treasures upon earth, where moth and rust doth corrupt, and where thieves break through and steal." (*Counsels on Stewardship*, p. 209)

Jesus also said, "Lay up for yourselves treasures in heaven" (Matt. 6:9). Is it wrong or sinful to work for your own interest? Is it wrong to have treasures? Look at Abraham, Solomon, Joseph, and Nicodemus—all were wealthy men. But what was their care? Compare that with the rich young ruler who was not willing to forsake all and follow Christ. Riches and self-sufficiency were his pollution.

The solution to the rich young ruler's pollution is as follows: "God does not condemn prudence and foresight in the use of the things of this life, but the feverish care, the undue anxiety, with respect to worldly things is not in accordance with His will" (*Counsels on Stewardship*, p. 159). The true Christian will use his or her abilities to serve God, not to please and glorify self.

Let's consider other pollution/solution situations.

Pollution      "The cares of this life and the greed for riches eclipse the glory of the eternal world" (*Testimonies for the Church*, vol. 4, p. 552).

Solution:      Think; "How worthless the reward the world offers beside that offered by our Heavenly Father" (*Counsels on Stewardship*, p. 227). Everything here is temporary. Eternal life with God and all His riches are permanent.

Pollution      "We have duties at home which cannot be neglected. But, all too often we become drunk with the cares of this life and they become a distraction. Work, hurry and drive are the order of the day, and our intense worldliness has its molding influence upon our children, the church, and upon the world" (*Testimonies for the Church*, vol. 4, p. 434).

Solution: Take time to be holy. The Word of God must not be neglected. Study, pray, study, and pray. "All who humble their hearts before Him will be taught of God.... The Lord wants every child to pray earnestly for wisdom, that they may know what the Lord would have him do. It is the privilege of every believer to obtain an individual experience, learning to carry his cares, distractions and perplexities to God" (Testimonies to Ministers and Gospel Workers, p. 478).

Pollution "When the love of the world takes possession of the heart and becomes a ruling passion, there is no room left for adoration to God" (*Testimonies for the Church*, vol. 3, p. 385). Remember, now, where it speaks of the heart, it is referring to the mind.

Solution: "When temptations assail you, when care, perplexity, and darkness seem to surround your soul, look to the place where you last saw the light. Rest in Christ's love and under His protecting care" (*The Ministry of Healing*, p. 250).

Pollution Guilt can be a destroyer of the soul. It is Satan's goal to hold everyone guilty and cause people to never feel forgiven.

Solution: The promise is in Jesus. "In whom we have redemption through His blood, even the forgiveness of sins" (Col. 1).

Pollution Unworthiness can prevent one from giving his or her life to Christ and cause an attitude of non-acceptance.

Solution:   "To the praise of the glory of His grace, wherein He hath made us accepted in the beloved" (Eph. 1:6). It is because of Jesus and His worthiness, which we accept as ours, that God will accept us as His, and count us worthy of salvation. Accepting Jesus gives us a worth more valuable than anything on earth.

Pollution   Restlessness.

Solution:   "When sin struggles for the mastery in the heart, when guilt oppresses the soul and burdens the conscience, when unbelief clouds the mind, remember that Christ's grace is sufficient to subdue sin and banish the darkness. Entering into communion with the Savior, we enter the region of peace" ( *The Ministry of Healing*, p. 250). "Come unto me, all ye that labor and are heavy laden and I will give you rest" (Matt. 11).

Pollution   Sin

Solution:   Whether you know it or not, you are weary and "heavy laden," or weighed down. "All are weighed down with burdens that only Christ can remove. The heaviest burden we bear is the burden of sin. If we were left to bear this burden, it would crush us" (*The Desire of Ages*, p. 328).

Pollution   Are you feeling crushed? Jesus can help if we ask Him. He will walk through the fire with us. Sin crushed Him. He bore the burden of guilt and weariness, the burden of cares, and the burden of sorrow. He bore the heaviest burden for us; He bore our sins.

Solution:  He carries us upon His heart. He watches over the trembling children of God. That includes you, friend. He is your only way out of this world alive.

| | |
|---|---|
| Are you tempted | He will deliver. |
| Are you weak | He will strengthen. |
| Are you ignorant | He will enlighten. |
| Are you wounded | He will heal. |
| Are you broken-hearted | He will mend. |

But you must surrender self before you can be delivered! "Whatever your anxieties and trials, spread out your case before the Lord. Your spirit will be braced for endurance" (*The Ministry of Healing*, p. 329)

Pollution  "There are causes for the present coldness and unbelief. The love of the world and the cares of life separate the soul from God" (*Testimonies for the Church*, vol. 3, p. 380).

Solution:  "... Jesus and heavenly things have altogether too small a share in our thoughts and affections. We should conscientiously discharge all the duties of everyday life, but it is also essential that we should cultivate, above everything else, holy affection for our Lord Jesus Christ" (*The Adventist Home*, p. 405).

Take to heart the following encouragement:

Be true, hopeful, heroic. Let every blow be made in faith. As you do your best, the Lord will reward your faithfulness. From the life-giving fountain draw physical, mental, and spiritual energy. Manliness,

womanliness—sanctified, purified, refined, enno-
bled—we have the promise of receiving…. As you fix
your eyes upon Him, you will be filled with a deep
love for the souls for whom He died, and will receive
strength for renewed effort. (*Selected Messages*, book 1,
p. 88)

Christ is our only hope. Please find your way to God in the name
of Jesus, who gave His life for you to be classified with Him. Amen.

See you in the clouds.

# Chapter Eleven

# Be The Attitude

It is said that life is not living without responsibility and attitude; consequently, to live a good life, one must accept responsibility and maintain the right attitude.

Have you ever wondered why the things that Jesus taught in the Sermon on the Mount were called the Beatitudes? In all of Scripture, this word is not mentioned even once; yet in many Bibles, such as the New King James Version, the supplied heading to introduce Matthew 5 reads, "The Beatitudes," in reference to verses 3-12. In reality it should be referring to all of chapters 5 through 7, inclusive. Throughout chapters 5 to 7, Jesus is teaching the importance of accepting responsibility and having the correct attitude to deal with things responsibly.

Jesus also teaches us that for every action, there is a reaction. As followers of Him, we are to guard our actions well so that we may promote the best possible reaction that will be for the good of all concerned. Then we can truly be joyful and "exceedingly glad."

You see, "blessed" and "happy" are those who mourn, not because they are mourning, but because they know they will be "comforted." Happy are those who hunger and thirst, because they know they will be "filled." This is about understanding God, knowing His truths and believing His promises. It will make you happy (blessed), and you will receive the rewards. Happy are those who are persecuted, for theirs is the reward of the kingdom of heaven.

In effect, Jesus is saying, "If you accept the responsibility of being a Christian and develop the right attitude toward God and your fellow men and women, you will be letting your light shine before them so they may see your good works and glorify your Father in heaven."

**Pause now:** Take some time and read Matthew chapters 5 to 7. You will discover what Jesus says is but an extension of chapter 5, verses 3 to 12.

God does not want irresponsible people with lousy attitudes to tend with for all eternity. He wants us to "change our minds" and put on the mind of Christ, to be like Him. Then He will liken you to the wise man who built his house on a rock and whose house did not fall.

In the classroom on the side of the mountain, Jesus was teaching us how to be successful Christians. Accept responsibilities, maintain the proper attitude, and do things responsibly. Resist evil and love God more than anyone, anything, any time, any place.

Compare this with Matthew 5:48: "Therefore you shall be perfect, just as your Father in heaven is perfect" (NKJV). What? Be like Him! How? When we formulate the decision to accept Jesus and make the effort to demonstrate in our lives God's will, Jesus will do a makeover in our lives, and by His stripes we are healed (1 Pet. 2:24).

Many today teach salvation without obligation, but Jesus says, "Not everyone that saith unto Me, Lord, Lord, shall enter into the kingdom of heaven; but he that doeth the will of My Father which is in heaven" (Matt. 7:21).

Jesus taught: Blessed are they who love God, for they will do unto others as I have done and will show Me love by keeping My commandments. Yes, friends; attitude, happiness, responsibility, love, hardship, and obedience are synonymous with Jesus.

How are you classified?

As you look into the Scriptures in Matthew 5 concerning the Beatitudes, how do you see yourself?

# ✦ Classified ✦

You can measure yourself with respect to these attitudes on a scale of one to four, with *one* representing a need for improvement, and *four* achieving your goal. Use the following statements to rate yourself.

Poor in Spirit
1 2 3 4

I have come to understand that I am accepted by God even when I find myself most unacceptable, in light of His love and forgiveness. I recognize my need for God and know that I do not have to earn His love with wealth, status, or spiritual sophistication.

Mourn
1 2 3 4

I have come to understand where I can really fill the empty places in my life. I can let others know when I am hurting and share my grief with others without embarrassment. I can weep as Jesus did.

Meekness
1 2 3 4

I understand that I do not have to be the martyr or strong person all the time. I can be tender and gentle with others. Winning is not always being first. I have given the control of my life over to God, and I do not have to be first all the time.

Hunger and Thirst for
Righteousness
1 2 3 4

I now understand that I want to know God and His will for my life more than anything. I am more excited about God's will for my life than my own financial gain, success in my career, or acceptance of my peers. I long for God's perspective in my decisions.

# Be The Attitude

Merciful

1 2 3 4

I understand that I can enter into the feelings of someone who is hurting, lonely, or distressed and feel the pain of their emotions. God has given me sensitivity for the suffering of others and the ability to exercise compassion on them.

Pure

1 2 3 4

I understand I can be completely open and honest with God. My thinking is more of Him and His ways rather than of me and mine. I do not have to pretend to be what I am not. I am learning to become transparent so Jesus is visible in everything I do and say.

Peacemaker

1 2 3 4

I have come to understand where I can really work at keeping the channels of communication open with those around me. I deal with anger and disagreements immediately and do not allow them to fester. I encourage people around me to work out their differences without hurting one another.

Persecuted

1 2 3 4

I understand what and whom I am living for, and for this cause I am not afraid to suffer and, if need be, die. I am willing to "take the heat" and stand with Jesus for what is right. I can take criticism without feeling self-pity or self-righteousness.

Verbally Abused /
Misrepresented

1 2 3 4

I have come to understand that those who hate God are liars and accusers under the influence of Satan. When someone speaks falsely of me, I can still be glad in the truth of God.

Having now classified yourself, please understand that no matter what your position in the race, if you are running with Jesus, you are a winner. To win with Jesus, you cannot stand still; you must keep advancing to the next step.

# Chapter Twelve

# Through The Fire

Oh yes, King David knew what it was like to suffer trials. But did he bring most of them upon himself? We humans have a tendency to do that, don't we? But what made the difference in David's life that enabled him to finally be victorious?

David understood repentance and forgiveness and his need to depend upon God. In spite of his sinful acts, David was a man after God's own heart. However, God had to refine David with the fires of trials.

Did you know that each fiery trial is God's agent for refining? Even when we bring trouble upon ourselves, God is there to purify us. Remember the three Hebrew slaves in the Book of Daniel? Their victory over the image did not just happen by way of circumstance. The image that they refused to worship was the golden idol that represented Nebuchadnezzar. After this incident, Nebuchadnezzar would not turn his will and his mind to God, and he became like a beast. The consequence of not bowing down to the image was the death penalty. Does this situation sound familiar to you? The Bible tells us that just before Jesus returns, there will be a death penalty for those who do not bow and worship the beast and its image. A deeper, personal study of this subject will be helpful to you.

The victory of the Hebrew slaves did not just happen; the Hebrew slaves had to prepare for it. They were slaves, equal to a life of trials and temptations. They were torn from their native land, and yet nobody could break their relationship with God. Their demonstration was a defiance of the earthly, human powers that opposed God's principles. All the trials and hardships they experienced are what prepared and developed their characters for victory. God rewarded them by standing with them and delivering them.

The Bible does not tell us that life is going to be without suffering. To live a life with God, we have to suffer and pass through the fires of refinement. Furthermore, our Creator will stand by us and help us overcome the obstacles that stand between us and Him. Have you ever considered that what these oppressed Hebrews were experiencing is similar to what we are facing today at the end of time? If you think so, then you are correct.

We need to recognize that our hardships in life are character builders. We should praise God for discipline and be thankful that He looks after His children. We need to have the right attitude, brothers and sisters.

The three Hebrew slaves went through the fires of life knowing God on a personal level through study and prayer. Consequently, they were ready when the big test came. Jesus says that He will stand by us when we are tested in the fire. Moreover, all of us will be refined as gold is refined and purified in the fire.

But keep in mind that there is a fire that we do not want in our lives. The fire we do not want in our lives is called a backfire. Backfire is a process firefighters use in a forest fire. They start a smaller fire that burns toward the larger fire, and when it reaches the larger fire, it leaves nothing in the path of the larger fire to burn so it is extinguished. This can be a good strategy for the firefighters; however, a backfire can rebound and get out of hand, and the next thing you know, the fire is worse than when it started. Let me explain.

In the Christian life, when God's people get on fire for Him and things become ablaze, Satan starts a backfire to snuff out the flames. This backfire does not belong among God's people. It is by our carelessness, our indifference, our unkind words, and selfish acts toward one another that Satan builds these backfires. These fiery darts are intended solely to put out the flame of the Holy Spirit. Oftentimes we do not recognize that it is us Satan is using to quench the fire not only of others but also in ourselves.

Furthermore, the dangers of backfire are why personal prayer and study are so important. Preparation for the fire of the Holy Spirit and the victories of the fiery tests draw us nearer to God. We need to earnestly seek the Lord every moment of our lives. Oh, brothers and sisters, the Christian life is a life of fire. I pray that God will set us ablaze and give us understanding.

In order for us to be successful overcomers and be burning lights for Him, Jesus wants us to purchase three things found in Revelation 3:18:

1. **EYE SALVE** – Eye salve symbolizes understanding and discernment by way of the Holy Spirit. He is the eye salve! The more we learn about God, the more we understand. It is the Holy Spirit who teaches us and opens our understanding. So as we go through trials and hardships, we need to pray for the Holy Spirit to come into our lives and help us grasp what is happening. He will give us understanding of and through the Word. Study the Bible and learn about Jesus. The Holy Spirit's eye salve will help you to see things as Jesus does and to walk through the fire with Him. How do you obtain the Holy Spirit? All you have to do is ask for Him to come into your life. Moreover, study and pray to reinforce your understanding.

2. **WHITE RAIMENT** – White raiment, or a white robe, is a recurring symbol of Christ's righteousness. White is the

purity, or the sinlessness, of Jesus. The raiment is the covering that He provides to hide our shame. Shame is our sins. Jesus covers us with Himself and makes us whiter than snow. If you want to live with God, you have to be purely sinless, and the only one who can provide that for you is Jesus Christ, our Savior and Lord. That is why He is called the Savior. How do you get the white raiment of Jesus so that you can enter into the gates of heaven? You have to fall in love and get married! Jesus is the groom, and we can be the bride. So fall in love, marry Him, and obtain righteousness. Furthermore, your name will be recorded in the book of life, in the name of Jesus Christ, and you are re-classified. However, remember, being married to Jesus may cause you to face trials and hardships. He is going to test your love and loyalty. You are going to be put through the fire. Sometimes you may feel like leaving Jesus, but do not go by your own feelings; pray for the eye salve of understanding. Trust in Him. He will provide a way of escape.

3.  **GOLD BY FIRE** – The symbol of gold refined by fire teaches us that Jesus will take any old gold there is, impurities and all. However, Jesus takes us through a purification process so that we will be fine gold for His eternal kingdom. He will melt us down and scrape off impurities from the top. Sometimes we have to humble ourselves and be willing to go through the trials of being melted down so that we can be reshaped. Jesus wants to reshape and purify our characters. Consequently, the gold represents our refined characters of faith, purified by the fires of trials and hardships in our lives that give us the opportunity to demonstrate our love and loyalty to our Bridegroom. Jesus is our golden opportunity for eternal life. Please give Him permanent residency in your life.

Jesus uses trials in our lives to

- bring light to undiscovered traits of character,
- cleanse us from earthliness and selfishness, and
- correct our defective disposition and mannerisms.

He allows trials into our lives to

- remove sharp corners of character,
- build trust in Him,
- educate, train, and discipline us to develop our character, and purify and prepare us to receive His seal of ownership.

He permits us to go through the fire because it is what

- brings us nearer to Him,
- causes Christ's image to be perfectly reflected in us, and
- prepares us for the accomplishment of His purpose for us.

How we react to our trials of fire is what

- creates a distinction between Christians and worldly people, and
- helps fit us for heaven (life) or hell (death).

Brothers and sisters, God calls for complete and entire consecration; anything short of this can cause separation. Complete consecration is expected in any marriage. The more difficult your position, the more you need Jesus.

I tell you in the fear of God, your path is beset by dangers that you do not see and do not realize. You will go through the fire if you give your life to Jesus. Even if it seems as if you are all alone, Jesus is there! You must hide in Him! You must cling to Him! Your life is in jeopardy unless you hold the hand of Christ.

If you want to be refined to pure gold, you have to buy from the Bridegroom. You have to buy the eye salve and you must receive the white raiment. Being married to Jesus is your decision. Christ has already chosen you, but will you choose and cling to Him? You have to reach out your arms, clasp hands with Him, and walk through the fire with Him. Our buying power is wrought through the decisions we make. We buy from Jesus with decision and commitment.

Seek Jesus in prayer. Make a commitment; say it to yourself and say it to Him. Do not make promises that you cannot keep, but accept His promises. Make decisions and set goals. But if you must make a promise, let it be to pledge yourself to Him.

If you want to be satisfied, then with Him you must be classified.

Our mission in life is to find love, decide where we are going to spend eternity, and help others do the same, but you have to walk through the fire if you want to spend eternity in heaven with Jesus Christ. Make a choice today and turn your will and your life over to the hands of our Lord Jesus Christ. You can find Him in prayer and the Word. God will put you on higher ground if you let Him. Ask for Christ to come into your heart today while you are still breathing. Make a commitment and marry Jesus no matter what, in comparison, heaven will not be as expensive for you as it was for Jesus and He's waiting to share His dowery with you.

CLASSIFIED with Him, is the only way to LIFE .

*What If?*

What if we treated our Bible like we do our cell phone?

What if we carried it around in our pockets or purses?

What if we flipped through it several times a day?

What if we turned back to get it if we forgot it?

What if we used it to receive messages from text to text?

What if we treated it like we couldn't live without it?

What if we gave it to kids as gifts?

What if we used it when we traveled?

What if we used it in case of an emergency?

What if we went, "Hmmm, where is my Bible?"

What if we didn't have to worry about being disconnected?

What if Jesus paid the bill?

What if there were no more dropped calls?

What if there was a message for you every day?

What if you never lost the signal?

What if you had to replace it because it was worn out?

WOULD IT STILL BE DUSTY?

# About the Author

A third-generation Seventh-day Adventist, Bly Beamesderfer is a retired general construction contractor, he remains active as a handyman.

In addition to working with his hands, Bly serves the Lord traveling and presenting inspirational programs at which he sings and offers his testimony as an encouragement to others. Bly has produced a CD titled *Jesus and Me.*

We invite you to view the complete
selection of titles we publish at:

**www.TEACHServices.com**

Scan with your mobile
device to go directly
to our website.

Please write or email us your praises, reactions, or
thoughts about this or any other book we publish at:

# TEACH Services, Inc.
P U B L I S H I N G
www.TEACHServices.com • (800) 367-1844

P.O. Box 954
Ringgold, GA 30736

**info@TEACHServices.com**

TEACH Services, Inc., titles may be purchased in bulk for
educational, business, fund-raising, or sales promotional use.
For information, please e-mail:

**BulkSales@TEACHServices.com**

Finally, if you are interested in seeing
your own book in print, please contact us at

**publishing@TEACHServices.com**

We would be happy to review your manuscript for free.

www.ingramcontent.com/pod-product-compliance
Lightning Source LLC
Chambersburg PA
CBHW060546100426

42742CB00013B/2470